Multinationalism and Covid-19

Edited by
André Lecours and Stephanie Kerr

LONDON AND NEW YORK

First published 2023
by Routledge
4 Park Square, Milton Park, Abingdon, Oxon OX14 4RN

and by Routledge
605 Third Avenue, New York, NY 10158

Routledge is an imprint of the Taylor & Francis Group, an informa business

Introduction, Chapters 1, 3 and 4 © 2023 Taylor & Francis
Chapter 2 © 2021 Karlo Basta and Ailsa Henderson. Originally published as Open Access.
Conclusion © 2023 Stephanie Kerr

With the exception of Chapter 2, no part of this book may be reprinted or reproduced or utilised in any form or by any electronic, mechanical, or other means, now known or hereafter invented, including photocopying and recording, or in any information storage or retrieval system, without permission in writing from the publishers. For details on the rights for Chapter 2, please see the chapter's Open Access footnote.

Trademark notice: Product or corporate names may be trademarks or registered trademarks, and are used only for identification and explanation without intent to infringe.

British Library Cataloguing in Publication Data
A catalogue record for this book is available from the British Library

ISBN13: 978-1-032-43070-6 (hbk)
ISBN13: 978-1-032-43072-0 (pbk)
ISBN13: 978-1-003-36560-0 (ebk)

DOI: 10.4324/9781003365600

Typeset in Minion Pro
by Newgen Publishing UK

Publisher's Note
The publisher accepts responsibility for any inconsistencies that may have arisen during the conversion of this book from journal articles to book chapters, namely the inclusion of journal terminology.

Disclaimer
Every effort has been made to contact copyright holders for their permission to reprint material in this book. The publishers would be grateful to hear from any copyright holder who is not here acknowledged and will undertake to rectify any errors or omissions in future editions of this book.

Contents

Citation Information		vi
Notes on Contributors		vii
	Introduction Multinationalism and the COVID-19 Pandemic: A Framework for Analysis	1
	André Lecours and Stephanie Kerr	
1	Multinationalism in the Spanish Territorial Debate during the COVID-19 Crisis. The Case of Catalonia and Intergovernmental Relations	17
	Marc Sanjaume-Calvet and Mireia Grau Creus	
2	Multinationalism, Constitutional Asymmetry and COVID: UK Responses to the Pandemic	37
	Karlo Basta and Ailsa Henderson	
3	Nationalism and COVID in Belgium: A Surprisingly United Response in a Divided Federal Country	55
	Dave Sinardet and Jade Pieters	
4	Trumpist Ethnonationalism and the Federal Response to the COVID-19 Crisis and Other Natural Disasters in Puerto Rico (2017–21)	75
	Jaime Lluch	
	Conclusion Looking Forward: Multinationalism and Responses to Covid-19	94
	Stephanie Kerr	
	Index	102

Citation Information

The following chapters were originally published in the journal *Nationalism and Ethnic Politics*, volume 27, issue 3 (2021). When citing this material, please use the original page numbering for each article, as follows:

Introduction

Multinationalism and the COVID-19 Pandemic: A Framework for Analysis
André Lecours and Stephanie Kerr
Nationalism and Ethnic Politics, volume 27, issue 3 (2021), pp. 257–272

Chapter 1

Multinationalism in the Spanish Territorial Debate during the COVID-19 Crisis. The Case of Catalonia and Intergovernmental Relations
Marc Sanjaume-Calvet and Mireia Grau Creus
Nationalism and Ethnic Politics, volume 27, issue 3 (2021), pp. 273–292

Chapter 2

Multinationalism, Constitutional Asymmetry and COVID: UK Responses to the Pandemic
Karlo Basta and Ailsa Henderson
Nationalism and Ethnic Politics, volume 27, issue 3 (2021), pp. 293–310

Chapter 3

Nationalism and COVID in Belgium: A Surprisingly United Response in a Divided Federal Country
Dave Sinardet and Jade Pieters
Nationalism and Ethnic Politics, volume 27, issue 3 (2021), pp. 311–330

Chapter 4

Trumpist Ethnonationalism and the Federal Response to the COVID-19 Crisis and Other Natural Disasters in Puerto Rico (2017–21)
Jaime Lluch
Nationalism and Ethnic Politics, volume 27, issue 3 (2021), pp. 331–349

For any permission-related enquiries please visit:
www.tandfonline.com/page/help/permissions

Notes on Contributors

Karlo Basta is Lecturer in Politics at the University of Edinburgh, UK. He works on the comparative politics of nationalism, with a focus on multinational states. He is the author of *The Symbolic State: Minority Recognition, Majority Backlash, and Secession in Multinational Countries* (2021).

Mireia Grau Creus works at the Institut d'Estudis Autonòmics, Government of Catalonia. She holds a PhD in Political and Social Sciences from the European University Institute, Florence, Italy. Her research interests focus on intergovernmental relations, federalism, and multi-level governance.

Ailsa Henderson is Professor of Political Science at the University of Edinburgh, UK. She conducts research on political culture(s) and political behaviour in federal and multinational states and focuses in particular on variations in political culture at the sub-state level. Her publications explore how national identity, federalism, devolution, or institutional design can affect regional variations in political attitudes and behaviours.

Stephanie Kerr is Assistant Professor at the Department of Political Science, University of Lethbridge, Canada. Her research specialization focuses primarily on nationalism, political violence, and multi-level governance, with a regional focus on Western Europe and Latin America.

André Lecours is Professor in the School of Political Studies at the University of Ottawa, Canada. His main research interests are nationalism and federalism. His most recent book is *Nationalism, Secessionism, and Autonomy*.

Jaime Lluch is Professor at the Department of Political Science, University of Puerto Rico (RP). He is a comparativist who works on the constitutional and political accommodation of national diversity in multinational democracies, comparative federalism, migration and citizenship in comparative perspective, European and EU politics, and comparative public law.

Jade Pieters is Political Advisor at the Embassy of the Netherlands in Brussels. He holds a master's degree in Political Science from the Free University of Brussels (VUB), Belgium. He interned at the Permanent Representation of Belgium to the United Nations.

Marc Sanjaume-Calvet is Assistant Professor at the Department of Political and Social Sciences, Universitat Pompeu Fabra.Mireia, Spain. His research interests include Federalism, Secession, Cultural Justice, Social Justice, and Democracy. His research has been published in the *Journal of Politics*, *Party Politics*, *Nations and Nationalism*, *Canadian Journal of Political Science* and *Representation* among others.

Dave Sinardet is Professor of Political Science at the VUB (Free University of Brussels), Belgium and teaches a course in the multilingual program of the Université Saint-Louis in Brussels. His main research interests are (sub state) nationalism, federalism, multi-level politics and multilingual public spheres. He is also an expert on Belgian politics and on Belgium's constitutional reform process.

Introduction

Multinationalism and the COVID-19 Pandemic: A Framework for Analysis

André Lecours and Stephanie Kerr

ABSTRACT

The introduction to the special issue offers a six-points framework for analyzing both the impact of the pandemic on nationalism and the broader multinational state as well as the significance of multinationalism for the response to the pandemic. These points correspond to the following questions: (1) How has multinationalism (as a sociological fact and/or a political culture that has conditioned governance practices and institutional frameworks) shaped the response to the crisis? (2) How has the crisis affected the self-determination objectives and strategies of the nationalist movement? (3) Have national divides (as observed, for example, in public opinion and in statements from politicians) become more or less salient during, and as a result of, the crisis? (4) What issues have produced tensions between national communities, or between minority nations and the state? (5) What governments, parties, or individual politicians have most gained or lost from the crisis in terms of putting forward or managing self-determination claims? (6) What could be the impact of the crisis on the nationalist movement and on the multinational state as a whole?

Introduction

Nationalist movements represent fundamental political forces in the politics of several liberal-democratic states. These multinational democracies[1] operate fundamentally differently from mononational ones insofar as questions related to the nature of the *demos*, the legitimacy of government action, and even the territorial integrity of the state tend to hover over the entirety of politics. Moreover, multinational democracies tend to be federal or decentralized states,[2] which means that they also often involve relationships between governments that are tinted by different national projects. Hence, multinational democracies involve conflictual territorial dynamics between, on the one hand, "minority nations," and, on the other hand, the state and its own (majority) nationalism, which typically takes hold in the rest of the country.[3] Politics in these democracies are strongly conditioned by this dynamic relationship.

As such, exogeneous forces, insofar as they impact nationalism (minority as well as majority), present important potential for altering multinational democracies. Moreover, multinationalism as a fundamental condition of some states seems likely to shape the political and public policy response to these types of forces. Wars represent one such exogenous force whose impact on nationalism and multinational democracies has been analyzed, whether it be for how they centralized Canadian federalism[4] or facilitated the de-legitimization of Flemish nationalism.[5] Global economic crises (and related politics and policies of austerity) are another, and they have been studied for their effects on nationalist movements in minority nations such as Québec, Scotland, and Catalonia[6] as well as for their impact on the territorial structuring of multinational states.[7] The COVID-19 pandemic represents a massive exogenous force for which there is little to no precedent.

A little over two months after the Chinese government issued a statement about a "pneumonia" outbreak in Wuhan, the World Health Organization declared a global pandemic on 11 March 2020. This pandemic would be a shock of gigantic proportion for all states and their citizens, a public health crisis without precedent in the past 100 years. For example, while the SARS outbreak (2002–2004) had a much higher case fatality rate[8] (9.6% to COVID-19's 2.1%), there were only 8,096 confirmed cases of SARS, with 774 deaths. Over the (to date) shorter period between December 2019 and early June 2021, there were 171 million confirmed cases of COVID-19 worldwide resulting in a staggering 3.5 million deaths.[9]

Highlighting the role of local contexts[10] and policy decisions, both the number of cases as well as fatality rates varied significantly between states as well as between regions within states, a potentially significant reality in multinational countries. For instance, as of 31 May 2021, the United Kingdom had reported 4,484,060 cases (6,709 cases per 100,000 inhabitants) whereas in Scotland there were 4,318 cases per 100,000 inhabitants (although the fatality rate was higher in Scotland than in the United Kingdom as a whole, 3.2% compared to 2.8%).[11] As of 1 June 2021, Belgium had a COVID-19 fatality rate of 2.3%, Spain's was 2.2%, and the United States' was 1.8%.[12]

This special issue is dedicated to assessing, through case studies, both the impact of the pandemic on nationalism and the broader multinational state as well as the significance of multinationalism for the response to the pandemic. More specifically, the authors tackle one or more of the following six questions: (1) How has multinationalism (as a sociological fact and/or a political culture that has conditioned governance practices and institutional frameworks) shaped the response to the crisis? (2) How has the crisis affected the self-determination objectives and strategies of the nationalist movement? (3) Have national divides (as observed, for example, in public opinion and in statements from politicians) become more or less salient during, and as a result of, the crisis? (4) What issues have produced tensions between national communities, or between minority nations and the state? (5) What governments, parties, or individual politicians have most gained or lost from the crisis in terms of putting forward or managing self-determination claims? (6) What could be the impact of the crisis on the nationalist movement and on the multinational state as a whole? The case studies used to sort through these questions are Catalonia and Spain; Scotland and the United Kingdom; Flanders and Belgium; and Puerto Rico and the United States.

The following section discusses to the aforementioned questions on the relationship between the COVID-19 pandemic and nationalism. Then, we introduce the articles of this special issue.

Multinationalism and the pandemic: some categories of analysis

An analysis of the relationship between the COVID-19 pandemic and multinationalism can be conducted through several different angles. Here are six important questions that can help tease out the dynamics of the pandemic in multinational democracies.

(1) How has multinationalism shaped the response to the crisis?

As Bieber[13] points out, little work has been done on the relationship between pandemics (as well as other forms of natural disasters) and nationalism. This is all the more true with respect to the interplay between such crises and not only nationalist movements but also the broader multinational context.

The role of identity in times of crisis can involve bringing once acrimonious communities together by redefining or reinforcing group boundaries as they face a common challenge. In the case of nationalist movements, this could mean reinforcing the boundaries of the minority nation (as has happened in Catalonia, Scotland, and Puerto Rico) or it could feature momentum toward an expansion of national boundaries to the level of the state on the basis of a shared experience with the rest of the country (surprisingly, a dynamic found in Belgium, as explained by Sinardet and Pieters). The nature of this reaction to the challenge of the pandemic, whether driven by the nationalist leadership or reflective of societal dynamics, can have important repercussions on the relationship between central and minority nation governments.

The particular institutional mechanisms in place to accommodate the presence of multiple nations within a state may strengthen narratives about the importance of autonomy, both when those institutions respond well and when they are found wanting. The key tension here is between, on the one hand, the centralizing instincts of central governments in times of crisis or, at least, their preferences for coordination across regional governments (including the government of minority nations) and, on the other hand, these governments developing a more autonomous and locally-tailored response.

For those states whose multinational character is reflected in the design of their territorial structuring, the response to the crisis could be funneled through regional governments. Yet, central governments can be expected to want to play some directive, coordination or at least supervisory role since strongly structuring the response to a pandemic along internal borders may seem antithetical to tackling an essentially borderless problem. Hence, questions of coordination between the governments of minority nations, their neighbors, and the central government become paramount to developing an effective response to the crisis. In their article, Sinardet and Pieters note that public support for a more coordinated response at times put limits on Flemish attempts to implement distinctive measures. But, of course, the governments of minority nations may wish to keep such coordination to a minimum in order to be able to truly act autonomously. In this regard, the multinational character of a state paired with significant decentralized powers over not only health care but also public health more broadly and the regulation of the economy involves a political (and policy) response whose balance is particularly delicate.

Indeed, the central government may find itself in a position wherein attempts to implement its preferred approach are met with resistance from minority nations looking for a more locally-tailored response or unwilling to see funds and other resources move out of the region, as the central government looks to redistribute supplies and resources to the areas most in need across the country. If the relationship between the two levels of government is acrimonious, the ability of the central government to coordinate its response to the pandemic across the country is likely to be hampered, as the case of the United States tends to demonstrate. This result—or even the possibility of this result—may lead to the central government pushing for, and perhaps succeeding in, re-centralizing political power. Sanjaume-Calvet and Grau Creus have seen this type of dynamic in the case of Catalonia with Spain where the idea that the virus does not respect borders has been used by the central government to support a centralized response to the pandemic, an argument that becomes particularly powerful in the absence of a strong *culture* of multinationalism. In other words, and as the article by Basta and Henderson suggests, multinationalism as a sociological fact may be less important than multinationalism as a political culture for understanding the response of multinational democracies to the virus. Of course, the degree to which regional governments are constitutionally protected, the capacity of the central government to undertake constitutional amendments,[14] and the ability of this government to withhold or attach conditions to funding and fiscal transfers all impact the ease with which state recentralization can be undertaken in the name of improving coordination and policy response more broadly.

For minority nations with autonomous powers of note (for example, health care, public health, education, business regulation), there exists the possibility of localized responses that address specific needs and realities, especially if the central government chooses to refrain from increasing centralization. Sanjaume-Calvert and Grau Creus show that while the pandemic may not have provided a framework for building a self-determination roadmap, it nonetheless lent itself to grievance discourses aimed at the central state. In this context, the governments of minority nations may find themselves in a position to take credit for those policies that are positively received or effectively implemented, all the while shifting blame for ineffective responses to the central government by claiming the lack of necessary tools to adequately respond to the crisis. This may be so regardless of whether issues with planning or implementation can objectively be laid at the feet of one or the other government. Credit-claiming and blame-shifting typically have little do to with objective facts,[15] as the Trump administration (and its ethno-nationalism, as Lluch explains in his article) amply demonstrated not only in relation to Puerto Rico but also to the continental United States. It is even more the case when governments can mobilize the powerful idea of the nation to promote their own action and criticize the policies of other governments. In turn, the politics of nationalist credit-claiming and blame-shifting (from either or both central and minority nations' governments) can lead to a less than optimal response to the pandemic. Basta and Henderson note that messaging on pandemic responses, rates, and measures in the UK suffered from a lack of clarity as to the territorial reach of any given announcement, for instance frequently failing to identify when measures applied only to England or to the UK as a whole.

(2) How has the crisis affected the self-determination objectives and strategies of the nationalist movement?

National identities are the result of social, political and discursive practices. Indeed, it has been well established that these identities are not fixed but rather fluid: "nationhood cannot be constructed and established once and for all, rather, national identities are continuously negotiated, co-constructed, reproduced, re-narrated" in accordance with the local and global socio-political context.[16] National identity is inherently relational:

there is no "us" without a "them."[17] What is more, as identity is a dynamic and fluid concept that is deeply grounded in a specific context—be it cultural, political, institutional, or geographic—drastic changes in such context, such as those posed by a crisis on the scale of the current pandemic, afford nationalist movements the opportunity to revisit the boundaries of "us" and "them," reinforcing or recalibrating what membership in the group means. In turn, such reexamination of membership in national communities (potentially both the nation promoted by the state and the minority nation) may have implications for the nationalist movement's objectives (independence, increased autonomy, or some other change to the state's constitutional and institutional structure) and for the strategies used to attain these objectives.

The strategic nature of this opportunity has not been lost on the leadership of some nationalist movements. The pandemic, and the responses from the central and minority nation's governments (and especially the contrast between the two), provides an opportunity not only to highlight the difference with the "other" but also to make the case for the importance of more significant decentralization or even independence. Should the central government's attempts at a coordinated response to the pandemic be experienced as a curtailing of the normal powers of a minority nation's government, or even an attempt at recentralization, political leadership in the minority nation can easily choose to reinforce the boundaries between minority and majority nations. In short, the pandemic may translate into a stronger push for more radical self-determination options if the central government is viewed, or can be viewed, as having mismanaged the pandemic. In the Catalan case, the Sanjaume-Calvet and Grau Creus article notes that an increase in cases after the return of autonomy to the Autonomous Community following an initially centralized response was framed by the Catalan government and its supporters as meaning that, while the Catalan government knew how to address the crisis, it required more resources and powers to do so effectively, optimally in the form of full statehood. A different dynamic emerged in Belgium where, as Sinardet and Pieters explain, the uniform Belgian response sought and designed by the traditional (Flemish and Francophone) parties placed the Flemish nationalist party *Nieuw-Vlaamse Alliantie* (N-VA) in a tricky political situation.

Where coordination between multiple levels of government facilitated the relatively effective delivery of services and the adoption of measures, underwritten and facilitated by the central government's resources and organizations, it is likely that the narrative coming from the central government will focus on the effectiveness of the existing division of powers and the risk-pooling benefits for the minority nation to remain part of the state. In the face of an overall pandemic management viewed as effective, two main strategic options are available to nationalist movements. First, if this effectiveness is seen as evidence of the success of the current institutional arrangements, it may be used by a nationalist party (particularly one that may have been in power for some time) as evidence of the benefits yielded by their work advocating on behalf of the minority nation. In turn, such a nationalist party may use the perceived competent management of the pandemic to boost support for itself, if not its project. Second, this competent management could also be highlighted by the nationalist parties as evidence that they have the know-how and that their government has the institutional capacity to successfully address any and all situations. This type of discourse could be used to defend an existing autonomy in the face of a central government looking to retrench the powers of the minority nation's government or to argue that this government should be entrusted with an even greater degree of responsibility, even independent statehood.

The complex and transnational character of the pandemic may also serve to highlight the importance of cooperation across and between states. For some nationalist movements, the pandemic may mean advocating for a greater role internationally, on the basis of increased autonomy, or strategically stepping back under the wing of the central government to use the state's greater negotiating power when it so suits. In this context, if the state's response was seen relatively favorably—even if only for the state as a whole and not for the minority nation specifically—this could take the form of a renewed push by the minority nation's government to participate in the state's international effort at, for example, procurement. If the response of the state was generally seen as sub-optimal, a new or renewed emphasis on the international arena (through paradiplomacy),[18] presumably for the purpose of improving responsiveness to a pandemic, can represent a way for the minority nation's government to emphasize distinctiveness and autonomy from the central state by attempting to bypass the state and exercise agency abroad.[19] Alternatively, the minority nation's government can look to be seen as aiding the central government to better respond to a crisis by pushing for the state's increased involvement in multilateral efforts around the pandemic response.

(3) Have national divides become more or less salient during and as a result of the crisis?

Krastev and Leonard[20] argue that in the early stage of the COVID-19 crisis "politics was suspended, and public opinion fell in behind the actions of national governments." Yet, as the crisis drew out, the leeway afforded to governments and political leaders shrunk. This may have helped drive twinned trends toward the reinforcement of discourses of difference as well as a debate on the nature of cooperation within and beyond the multinational state.

If moments of crisis are opportunities for the state to restructure,[21] then they are also moments for national identities themselves to be rewritten, adjusted, or simply reinforced. These possible changes to national identities in the midst of the collective anxiety of the pandemic present strong potential to make nationalism, whether in its minority or majority forms, more exclusionary.[22] This can involve a hardening of borders, both between regions within a state and between states, as well as increasingly charged rhetoric. From the minority nation, there may be a narrative focused on the central government as unhelpful, or even as an impediment to an effective response to the crisis. As Jaime Lluch explains, this was certainly the case in Puerto Rico, as the political leadership was almost unanimously critical of President Trump and the United States federal government for their management of the pandemic, as well as of previous crises, on the island.

In addition, the view, in minority nations, that the state is using the crisis to re-centralize may come with suggestions that such re-centralization is evidence of the untrustworthiness of the central government and the corresponding importance of greater autonomy or even of independence. Coming from the central government, the discourse may accuse the minority nation of political opportunism and of a betrayal for wanting to discuss or adjust autonomy in the midst of a pandemic. Such discourse may also involve pointing to autonomous institutions as impediments to effective coordination, providing a narrative justification for recentralization. As Sanjaume-Calvet and Grau Creus discuss in their contribution, both of these dynamics have been present in Spain, at least with respect to Catalonia.

(4) What issues have produced tensions between national communities or between minority nations and the state?

Given the importance of social media and the internet as a vehicle for collective discourse, including nationalist discourse,[23] particularly in a period of long-lasting lockdowns, tensions between national communities or between minority nations and the state are likely to have found abundant space for amplification and dissemination. From cries of interference, or neglect (or both) by the central government in relation to the minority nations, to central governments dismissing calls for more localized response in the name of a more integrated approach as happened in Spain (sometimes involving a rhetoric of ungrateful minority nationalists demanding special treatment as was the case in the United States for Puerto Rico), the highly politically, economically, and psychologically-charged nature of the pandemic and of its responses is filled with narratives competing for public attention.

Such tensions have arisen as a result of a host of contentious issues, including funding for pandemic responses and relief efforts; competing claims of authority to undertake such responses; the importance of locally-adapted solutions versus a centralized approach; travel between regions within a state; the closure of international borders; the opening and closure of businesses and schools; and the procurement and distribution of personal protective equipment and vaccines. In this context, Lluch's contribution illustrates the reticence of the Trump administration, fueled by majority nationalism, to federal funding obligations of crisis responses and pandemic relief efforts in Puerto Rico.

These tensions are, of course, not limited to multinational states but they are qualitatively, and perhaps also quantitatively, different in states where there is a significant nationalist movement because issues of autonomy and self-determination, and the arguments that can be made in favor of or against these two nationalist-related ideas, are always in the background. Tensions between national communities, or between minority nations and the state, can emerge not only in instances where it can be argued that a government has responded inappropriately. For instance, the government of a minority nation may have been able to respond with generally adequate policies, leading to an increase of its popularity that can potentially help its self-determination objectives down the road. Such a dynamic would unavoidably create tensions with the central government. Indeed, Basta and Henderson outline that while policy decisions taken by the Scottish government were largely similar to those taken by the central government, the Scottish government managed to differentiate itself through the timing of the policies, making the Scottish approach seem more prudent. Such an opportunity to stand out on the handling of the pandemic, they argue, has contributed to the increased level of support for Scottish independence witnessed throughout 2020.

In short, the question of authority and legitimacy in the crucial decisions that have to be made in an emergency situation such as the COVID-19 pandemic puts great stress on multi-national democracies. In their recent survey, Krastev and Leonard[24] found that Europeans were generally dissatisfied with the responses of their state governments. If this holds for those citizens who do not see the authority wielded over them by the central government as inherently problematic, it is very likely to be all the more pronounced in those minority nations that challenge the extent of centralization and the scope of policy action of the central government. For example, polls in Spain found that while an average of 73% of Spanish citizens would like to see the central government take a stronger role in the pandemic response, that number dropped to between 2.5% and 42% among supporters of nationalist parties in the Autonomous Communities of the Basque Country and of Catalonia.[25]

Beyond questions about the legitimacy of the authority on the basis of which pandemic responses are implemented, questions of funding responses are equally vulnerable to politicization in multinational democracies. In a multinational context, financial transfers are frequent sites of conflict, even outside times of crisis.[26] Contestation over the allocation of funds and resources is an often-central element to the narrative of nationalist movements—whether holding that minority nations overpay into state coffers and do not see services of comparable quality offered, or demanding greater transfers to the minority nation with greater control over how to spend such transfers.[27] This discourse is likely to be significantly exacerbated at a time when such a high degree of government intervention occurs, not only on public health but also on economic recovery and social assistance.

Finally, the imposition of limitations on domestic travel may be an issue of particular relevance in multinational states. For instance, on 20 November 2020, Scottish regulations limiting travel within Scotland, but also banning travel to any other part of the Common Travel Area,[28] as well as to England, Wales, and Northern Ireland, came into effect.[29] When it came time to lift restrictions in May 2021, Scotland also opted for a somewhat different approach than the rest of the UK.[30] Whereas, as of 24 May 2021, people in England were advised to minimize travel but in the absence of any legal restrictions, Scotland allowed travel within the UK but with the exception of designated hotspots in Scotland and parts of England. Generally speaking, these types of limitations in multi-national states may create conditions that could provide additional meaning to, and exacerbate existing tensions over, inter-state borders linked to federal or decentralized territorial structures. By reinforcing the borders between the minority nation and the rest of the country in an attempt to limit the transmission of the virus, the distinction between "us" and "them" along territorial lines is reinforced, with the "outsiders" now associated with the threat of bringing the virus with them.

(5) What governments, parties, or individual politicians have most gained or lost from the COVID-19 crisis in terms of putting forward or managing self-determination claims?

Nationalism is a form of politics and, as such, it is as much about political power as it is about identity. The extraordinary circumstances of the pandemic, which in minority nations such Catalonia, Flanders, Puerto Rico, and Scotland occurred as the politics of self-determination were in flux, can be expected to produce some political winners and losers on the very issue of self-determination. The pandemic offered political leaders, both within minority nations and at the central government, the opportunity to be highly visible.

The politicians of minority nations have been in a strong position to not only display leadership, but also to present their citizens with a (minority) nation-centric understanding of the way the pandemic and its response was unfolding in their community. Even when the policies adopted may not be remarkably different between minority nations and the rest of the country, questions of implementation, management, presentation, and communication can afford minority nationalist leadership a chance to stand out—or fail to—while under heightened scrutiny. There is a particular opportunity when the central government's leadership has been found wanting, as has been particularly the case in the United States and the United Kingdom. For instance, when it comes to Scotland and the United Kingdom, in a series of polls between May and August 2020, 74–82% of Scotts felt that First Minister Nicola Sturgeon was responding well or very well, compared to between 21% and 30% who felt that Prime Minister Boris Johnson could be said to be doing well or very well.[31] By October, Sturgeon was more popular in England than Johnson.[32] Across Great Britain, confidence in Johnson to make the right decisions with respect to the outbreak dropped from a high of a net confidence of 17% (calculated as the difference between the 56% of respondents having "a lot/fair amount" and 39% of respondents having "not very much/no" confidence) in April to fluctuating between a net confidence of −30% and −25% from late September 2020 into 2021. Meanwhile, across the same set of surveys, Sturgeon has held a relatively steady net confidence rating, hovering around +14%, with 49% having "a lot/fair amount" and 35% "not very much/no" confidence in her decision-making by late October of 2020.[33] In the 14 February 2021 Autonomous elections in Catalonia, nationalist parties maintained their absolute majority, but the significant change came in the near doubling of the seats held by the Socialist Party of Catalonia (PSC)—the regional sister party of the state governing Spanish Socialist Workers' Party (PSOE). PSC gained 16 seats to match the nationalist coalition partner Esquerra Republicana's (ERC) 33 seats, and it exceeded that of Junts per Catalunya's (JxCat) 32,[34] which may suggest a lack of appetite for radical constitutional change, at least in the immediate future.

In sum, the pandemic presents an opportunity for nationalist parties and their political class to acquire further leadership and management credibility, which can only help in furthering their self-determination project. At the same time, politicians from the central government can similarly gain popularity and respect through a management of the pandemic that citizens in minority communities find competent. In turn, acquiring a perhaps new-found positive standing may help them argue that the status quo works just fine and that self-determination claims are superfluous.

(6) What could be the impact of the crisis on the nationalist movement and on the multinational state as a whole?

The significance of a window such as the COVID-19 pandemic to demonstrate leadership and assert the importance of governing institutions can not only influence the political strength of specific political parties and political actors (both within and outside the minority nation), but it can also work to reshape the broader national identities. Alexander and Gao[35] note that national tragedies can act as a "symbolic vehicle" while Lee et al.[36] argue that "the discursive binding of a national community shines at critical moments or around special occasions that function as a reference point and furnish a rich repertoire of cultural symbols." The nature of the pandemic, specifically its impact on the whole of society regardless of whether or not an individual contracts the virus, leaves all the more space for the national community to participate in this discursive process. Eriksen[37] has argued that the internet can facilitate the diffusion of nationalist discourses and rhetoric while simultaneously facilitating communication, collaboration, and networking that allow for the narrative not only to be diffused but also adapted. In the context of the many stages of lockdown experienced across the world, the internet, social media, and public addresses by nationalist leaders, such as the televised briefings held by Scotland's Nicola Sturgeon, have been instrumental in laying out a narrative that reinforces the "togetherness" of the national community while highlighting differences with the central state. Of course, politicians operating at the central level have similarly attempted to emphasize the "togetherness" of the state-wide (majority) nation. In Belgium, as Sinardet and Pieters explain in their article, the De Croo government launched a campaign called "a team of 11 million" to try to promote this idea of Belgian "togetherness." Moreover, as Krastev and Leonard have suggested speaking on European integration, the pandemic may trigger "deeper anxiety about losing control in a dangerous world. It is about strengthening rather than weakening national sovereignty."

As such, much is still up in the air when it comes to the impact of the crisis on nationalist movements. Agency is important insofar as the actors who will be able to take better advantage of the leadership windows in these exceptional emergency circumstances may find themselves in an advantageous position on issues of self-determination. At the same time, institutional factors, considered in time, are also significant; if the momentum on autonomy within multinational democracies involves a *status quo* or, worst, retrenchment at a time when significant political parties in Catalonia, Flanders, Puerto Rico, and Scotland are seeking a re-negotiation of autonomous powers, secessionism could be significantly strengthened.[38]

With the outbreak of COVID-19 on a global scale, many predicted that the reinforcement of state borders as a means to prevent the spread of the virus would lead to a rise in nationalism,[39] particularly as the pandemic "began against a backdrop of strong mainstreamed exclusionary nationalism in key countries around the world, in particular in Europe and North America."[40] The high degree of health and economic interventions undertaken by governments has reinforced the primacy of the state,[41] putting renewed focus on the powers of governments at all levels. Sanjaume-Calvet and Grau Creus argue that the pandemic has produced not only a curtailing of momentum of the Catalan secessionist project, but also a closing of institutional pathways for territorial conflict resolution.

Yet, paradoxically, there were also predictions on a move toward increased cooperation between states as they were faced with a problem they could not solve on their own, with Rachman[42] arguing the pandemic has laid bare the ways in which individual states are vulnerable to global supply chain disruptions of key goods in times of crisis such as those that plagued the purchasing of personal protective equipment. If, as German Chancellor Angela Merkel has argued when announcing the Franco-German plan to raise €500bn to fund a European pandemic recovery plan "the nation state has no future standing alone,"[43] this risk may hold all the more true for the governments of minority nations. In this sense "shared geography dictates common action even more than shared values."[44] Nowhere is this tension between, on the one hand, the instinctive tightening of national communities and the reinforcing of national boundaries, and, on the other hand, the need for cooperation, more in evidence than in multinationalism democracies.

Presentation of the special issue

The articles of the special issue focus on Catalonia, Scotland, Flanders, and Puerto Rico, and on their respective multinational Spanish, British, Belgian, and American states. The first three countries are well recognized as multinational democracies[45] while the United States becomes multinational when considering its territorial possessions, first and foremost Puerto Rico.[46]

In all four of these multinational contexts, the politics of self-determination was prominent when the pandemic first hit in early 2020. In Catalonia, the so-called process was heading into an undetermined direction after the jailing of nationalist leaders and the offer by the Socialist-led Spanish government of a "table of negotiation." In Scotland, the exit of the United Kingdom from the European Union triggered a statement from First Minister Nicola Sturgeon about a second referendum on independence. In Flanders, both nationalist parties (N-VA and *Vlaams Belang*) had finished first and second respectively in the 2019 Belgian federal elections, paving the way for yet another long and difficult government formation process. Puerto Rico was heading toward a sixth referendum on status, this time involving a "yes/no" question on statehood in the American federation. The articles of the special issue explain the impact of the COVID-19 crisis on nationalism and these multinational democracies.

Sanjaume-Calvet and Grau Creus' article on Catalonia highlights the complexity of the impacts of the pandemic on governance in multinational contexts for the ways in which the existing institutional multinational framework produced pulls in seemingly two directions at once—toward the *status quo*, or even centralization, but also toward a hardening of already polarized positions within both sub-state nationalist and Spain-wide parties alike. Furthermore, they note the significant weight of the existing governance system in patterning both responses to the pandemic as well as the reactions of the state and of Catalan nationalist actors to those responses. While the crisis appeared to provide windows of opportunity for the Catalan nationalist project with respect to the articulation of grievances, the authors find that ultimately the overall impact has been roadblocks for the secessionist movement in terms of mobilization, stalled talks on the future of the relationship between Catalonia and the central state, and an increase in partisan polarization both within the movement itself, and between state and sub-state nationalists.

Focusing on the impact of majority nationalism on the pandemic response in the United Kingdom, Basta and Henderson examine how the relatively weak institutionalization of multi-level governance may have created a window of opportunity for the Scottish independence movement. By analyzing communications from Westminster and the resulting media coverage, the authors demonstrate an obfuscation of the territorial reach of given policies or announcements, as "UK" and "England" are frequently conflated. Furthermore, they note that the low level of salience of multi-level governance amongst UK political elites contributed to rather weak intergovernmental co-operation in response to the pandemic. Thus, the pandemic not only highlighted the lack of real acknowledgement of the UK's multi-level, and perhaps even multinational, character, but the absence of consideration of the autonomous nations has provided the Scottish government with an opportunity to stand out and to potentially further its self-determination agenda.

The article by Sinardet and Pieters discusses an unexpected outlier in terms of the response to the pandemic in the world of multinational states: Belgium, which showed a trend toward uniformity and coordination. Though the efficiency of decision-making was often hampered by the complex distribution of competencies (especially in health care), there was a significant public appetite for a coordinated, even a national, response in an otherwise politically and institutionally fragmented state typically exposed to strong centrifugal forces. This outcome is all the more surprising given that the early response to the crisis was led by a caretaker government that stemmed from yet another challenging government formation process. Under both this caretaker federal government and the regular federal government that was subsequently formed, the Belgian political class sought to reinforce and even set up common decision-making bodies in order to respond to the crisis. This approach put the Flemish nationalist party N-VA in a difficult situation, as it did not want to be seen to be obstructionist while at the same time remaining critical of Belgium and its governance. In sum, the pandemic unexpectedly saw the deployment of some form of banal Belgian nationalism that put Flemish nationalism somewhat on the defensive.

Finally, Lluch looks at the United States and Puerto Rico, emphasizing how the severity of the asymmetrical nature of the power relationship between the American federal government and Puerto Rico as an "unincorporated territory" left the island extremely vulnerable to the Trump administration's majority nationalism in times of crisis. This has meant that the response to the pandemic of the federal government in Puerto Rico has been characterized by discrimination and willful neglect stemming from the United States, and particularly the Trump administration, not conceptualizing Puerto Rico as a minority nation associated with the United States. Multinationalism is a sociological fact when it comes to the United States and Puerto Rico but it is not built into the American political culture. The mistreatment of the island by the American federal government during times of crises, including the pandemic, has led to changes in Puerto Rico, most importantly the rise in support for statehood, as Puerto Ricans search for a constitutional status that can bring about equality in the context of American citizenship. At the same time, the American mononational view greatly complicates any major adjustment in the relationship with Puerto Rico.

The pandemic is still ongoing, and so too are the relationships between nationalism and states outlined in this special issue. The articles of the special issue show not only a diversity of responses to the pandemic across cases but also the many different ways that the pandemic has impacted multinationalism and that multinationalism has affected the handling of the most severe public health crisis in generations. Such differentiation owes to specific constitutional and institutional contexts but also to political dynamics that were unfolding when COVID-19 first hit. Perhaps most significant for the immediate future of nationalist movements in Scotland, Catalonia, Flanders, and Puerto Rico is the fact that the effects of the pandemic have been felt differently in these minority nations. While the British response to the pandemic has arguably contributed to sustaining Scottish nationalism's drive toward another independence referendum, the Catalan nationalist movement (despite being met with efforts at recentralization by the Spanish state early on) has been unable to sustain its momentum, and it has also seen the narrowing of political pathways to bring the self-determination process to some sort of negotiated conclusion. In Flanders, the nationalist movement has also been puzzled by the pandemic since, for all its political culture and institutional history of fragmentation, Belgium developed a fair degree of uniformity and coordination in its response to COVID-19, leaving the N-VA and the broader Flemish nationalist movement trying to find a balance between assertiveness and cooperation (or, at least, non-obstruction). Puerto Ricans, for their part, faced a pandemic response heavily patterned by an emergent/resurgent majority American ethnonationalism that shirked the responsibilities of the United States toward its citizens on the island. The effect of this deployment of harsh majority nationalism on the statehood option for Puerto Rico remains to be seen.

Schertzer and Woods note that a particular crisis can act as a constitutive, amplifying, or transformative event in the development of nationalism.[47] This special issue starts with such a premise. It looks at the broad relationship between nationalist actors, state institutions, and political culture as well as at the particular dynamics of nationalism within specific multinational democratic states. Starting from a series of interwoven research questions laid out in this introduction, this special issue provides a framework for understanding the impact of not only COVID-19 but exogenous shocks more broadly on the ever dynamic and complex relationship between nationalism and state in multinational democracies.[48]

Notes

1. Alain-G. Gagnon and James Tully, eds., *Multinational Democracies* (Cambridge: Cambridge University Press, 2001); Michael Keating, *Plurinational Democracy. Stateless Nations in a Post-Sovereign Era* (Oxford: Oxford University Press, 2001); Alain-G. Gagnon, Montserrat Guibernau, and François Rocher, eds., *The Conditions of in Multinational Democracies* (Montreal and Kingston: McGill-Queen's University Press, 2003); André Lecours, Guy Laforest, and Nikola Brassard-Dion, eds., *Constitutional Politics in Multinational Democracies* (Montreal and Kingston: McGill-Queen's University Press, Forthcoming); Karlo Basta, *The Symbolic State. Minority Recognition, Majority Backlash, and Secession in Multinational Countries* (Montréal and Kingston: McGill-Queen's University Press, Forthcoming).
2. Michael Burgess and John Pinder, eds., *Multinational Federations* (London: Routledge, 2011).
3. Alain-G. Gagnon, André Lecours, and Geneviève Nootens, eds., *Contemporary Majority Nationalism* (Montreal and Kingston: Queen's University Press, 2011).
4. Garth Stevenson, *Unfulfilled Union. Canadian Federalism and National Unity*, 5th ed. (Montreal and Kingston: McGill-Queen's University Press, 2009).
5. Louis Vos, "The Flemish National Question," in *Nationalism in Belgium: Shifting Identities, 1780–1995*, edited by Kas Deprez and Louis Vos (New York: St. Martin's Press, 1998), 83–95.

6. Daniel Béland and André Lecours, "Nationalism and the Politics of Austerity: Comparing Catalonia, Scoland, and Québec," *National Identities* 23, no. 1 (2021): 41–57.

7. Diego Muro, "When Do Countries Re-Centralize? Ideology and Party Politics in the Age of Austerity," *Nationalism and Ethnic Politics* 21, no. 1 (2015): 24–43.

8. Calculated as the percentage of fatalities in reported cases.

9. The impact on health care systems and workers has been severe. One study of New York City health care workers during the first wave in the Spring of 2020 found that 57% of respondents screened positive for post-traumatic stress disorder (PTSD), 48% for major depression, and 33% for generalized anxiety disorder (Ari Shechter, Franchesca Diaz, Nathalie Moise, D. Edmund Anstey, Siqin Ye, Sachin Agarwal, Jeffrey L. Birk, Daniel Brodie, Diane E. Cannone, Bernard Chang, et al. "Psychological Distress, Coping Behaviours, and Preferences for Support among New York Healthcare Workers during the COVID-19 Pandemic," *General Hospital Psychiatry* 66 (2020): 1–8.).

10. Local contexts include population density, age and health; access to effective medical care; poverty and race.

11. The rates are calculated using data available from the Scottish National Health Service Data Set. It should be noted that as of 31 May 2021, two numbers are provided for deaths. The first, 7,669, is used to calculate the mortality rate. A second figure, 10,114, is also provided, and it includes any death certificates wherein COVID-19 is mentioned. The significant difference is illustrative of a much wider problem for ascertaining the data in relation to COVID-19.

12. Rates also varied significantly across cultural/ethnic communities within countries. In the United States, the Hispanic/Latino community accounts for only 18.45% of the population but, as of 1 June 2021, for 28.8% of cases (Centers for Disease Control and Prevention (CDC), "Demographic Trends of COVID-19 Cases and Deaths in the US Reported to CDC," 2020, https://covid.cdc.gov/covid-data-tracker/#demographics).

13. Florian Bieber, "Global Nationalism in Times of the COVID-19 Pandemic," *Nationalities Papers* (2020): 1–13.

14. Richard Albert, *Constitutional Amendments. Making, Breaking, and Changing Constitutions* (Oxford: Oxford University Press, 2019).

15. R. Kent Weaver, "The Politics of Blame Avoidance," *Journal of Public Policy* 6, no. 4 (1986): 371–98; R. Kent Weaver, "The Nays Have It: How Rampant Blame Generating Distorts American Policy and Politics," *Political Science Quarterly* 133, no. 2 (2018): 259–89.

16. Salma Kalim and Fauzia Janjua, "#WeareUnited, Cyber-Nationlism during Times of a National Crisis: The Case of a Terrorist Attack on a School in Pakistan," *Discourse & Communication* 12, no. 1 (2019): 68–94, 70.

17. Teun Adrianus Van Dijk, *Prejudice in Discourse an Analysis of Ethnic Prejudice in Cognition and Conversation* (Amsterdam and Philadelphia: J. Benjamins Pub. Co., 1984); Teun Adrianus Van Dijk, *Ideology: A Multidisciplinary Approach* (London: SAGE, 1998).

18. See Francisco Adelcoa and Michael Keating, eds., *Paradiplomacy in Action. The Foreign Relations of Subnational Governments* (London: Frank Cass, 1999).

19. André Lecours and Luis Moreno, "Paradiplomacy: A Nation-Building Strategy?," in *Conditions of Diversity in Multinational Democracies*, edited by Alain-G. Gagnon, Montserrat Guibernau, and François Rocher (Montréal: IRPP and McGill-Queen's University Press, 2003), 267–94.

20. Ivan Krastev and Mark Leonard, "Europe's Pandemic Politics: How the Virus Has Changed the Public's Worldview," *European Council on Foreign Relations* (2020). https://ecfr.eu/publication/europes_pandemic_politics_how_the_virus_has_changed_the_publics_worldview/

21. Bieber, "Global Nationalism in Times of the COVID-19 Pandemic."

22. Ibid.

23. Robert Schertzer and Eric Taylor Woods, "#Nationalism: The Ethno-Nationalist Populism of Donald Trump's Twitter Communication," *Ethnic & Racial Studies* 44, no. 7 (2021): 1154–1173.

24. Krastev and Leonard, "Europe's Pandemic Politics."

25. The significant variation corresponds to the positions with regard to autonomy and self-government, with the more autonomy-accepting Basque Nationalist Party (PNV) supporters representing the high of 42%, and the more independence-focused JxCat supporters representing the low of 2.5%; Carles Castro, "Catalunya y Euskadi ante la Covid-19" *La Vanguardia*, 4 April 2020, https://www.lavanguardia.com/politica/20200419/48600834822/gestion-crisis-sanitaria-cataluna-euskadi-torra-urkullu-gobierno.html.
26. François Boucher and Alain Noël, eds., *Fiscal Federalism in Multinational States. Autonomy, Equality and Diversity* (Montreal and Kingston: McGill-Queen's University Press, 2021).
27. Daniel Béland and André Lecours, *Nationalism and Social Policy. The Politics of Territorial Solidarity* (Oxford: Oxford University Press, 2008); Emmanuel Dalle Mulle, *The Nationalism of the Rich. Discourse and Strategies of Separatist Parties in Catalonia, Flanders, Northern Italy and Scotland* (London: Routledge, 2017).
28. United Kingdom, Republic of Ireland, Isle of Man, and Channel Islands.
29. Libby Brooks, 2020. "Covid Regulations Will Make it Illegal to Enter or Leave Scotland," *The Guardian*, 19 November 2020, https://www.theguardian.com/world/2020/nov/19/scotland-covid-regulations-will-make-it-to-enter-or-leave-country.
30. For both Northern Ireland and Wales, there are no travel restrictions for either the UK or the Common Travel Area, although Northern Ireland does have quarantining requirements for travel in the Common Travel Area.
31. "How Coronavirus Strengthened Scottish Independence," *The Economist*, 6 August 2020, https://www.economist.com/britain/2020/08/06/how-coronavirus-strengthened-scottish-independence; Glenn Campbell, "Covid: How the Coronavirus Pandemic is Redefining Scottish Politics," *BBC Scotland*, 22 September 2020, https://www.bbc.com/news/uk-scotland-scotland-politics-54250302.
32. Patrick Maguire and Greig Cameron, "Coronavirus in Scotland: Nicola Sturgeon More Liked in England than Boris Johnson," *The Sunday Times*, 24 October 2020, https://www.thetimes.co.uk/article/coronavirus-in-scotland-nicola-sturgeon-more-liked-in-england-than-boris-johnson-zqh0gvf20.
33. YouGov, "YouGov Coronavirus Handling Confidence Tracker," 7 January 2021, https://docs.cdn.yougov.com/ixbnz74wqx/YouGov_CoronaConfidence_Tracker_W.pdf.
34. El País, "Elecciones Catalanas," 15 February 2021, https://resultados.elpais.com/elecciones/2021/autonomicas/09/index.html.
35. Jeffrey Alexander and Rui Gao, "Remembrance of Things Past: Cultural Trauma, the 'Nanking Massacre' and Chinese Identity," in *Peking-Yale University Conference Publication on Tradition and Modernity: Comparative Perspectives* (Beijing: Beijing-Peking University Press, 2007), 266–94.
36. Lee CC, Pan Z, Chan JM, et al. "Through the Eyes of US Media: Banging the Democracy Drum in Hong Kong," *Journal of Communication* 51 (2001): 345–365.
37. Thomas Hylland Eriksen, "Nationalism and the Internet," *Nations and Nationalism* 13, no. 1 (2007): 1–17.
38. André Lecours, "Nationalism and the Strength of Secessionism in Western Europe: Static and Dynamic Autonomy," *International Political Science Review* (2020).
39. Bieber, "Global Nationalism in Times of the COVID-19 Pandemic."
40. Ibid., 4.
41. Gideon Rachman, "Nationalism is a Side Effect of Coronavirus," *Financial Times*, 23 March 2020, https://www.ft.com/content/644fd920-6cea-11ea-9bca-bf503995cd6f; Krastev and Leonard, "Europe's Pandemic Politics."
42. Rachman, "Nationalism is a Side Effect of Coronavirus."
43. Jennifer Rankin and Philip Oltermann, "Franco-German Plan for European Recovery Will Face Compromises," *The Guardian*, 26 May 2020, https://www.theguardian.com/world/2020/may/26/franco-german-plan-for-european-recovery-will-face-compromises.
44. Krastev and Leonard, "Europe's Pandemic Politics," 22.
45. Keating, *Plurinational Democracy*; Jaime Lluch, *Visions of Sovereignty: Nationalism and Accommodation in Multinational Democracies* (Philadelphia: University of Pennsylvania

Press, 2014); Dimitrios Karmis and François Rocher, *Trust, Distrust, and Mistrust in Multinational Democracies: Comparative Perspectives* (Montreal and Kingston: McGill-Queen's University Press, 2018).

46. Jaime Lluch, "The Legitimacy-Legality Constitutional Paradox in Multinational Democracies and the Constitutional Origins of Sub-State Party System Realignments," in *Constitutional Politics in Multinational Democracies*, edited by André Lecours, Nikola Brassard-Dion, and Guy Laforest (Montreal and Kingston: McGill-Queen's University Press, Forthcoming).

47. Eric Taylor Woods, Robert Schertzer, Liah Greenfeld, Chris Hughes, and Cynthia Miller-Idriss, "COVID-19, Nationalism, and the Politics of Crisis: A Scholarly Exchange," *Nations and Nationalism* 26, no. 4 (2020): 807–25.

48. Alan D. Kaye, Chikezie N. Okeagu, Alex D. Pham, Rayce A. Silva, Joshua J. Hurley, Brett L. Arron, Noeen Sarfraz, Hong N. Lee, G. E. Ghali, Jack W. Gamble, et.al. "Economic Impact of COVID-19 Pandemic on Healthcare Facilities and Systems: International Perspectives," *Best Practice & Research Clinical Anaesthesiology* (in press): 1–15. doi: 10.1016/j.bpa.2020.11.009; The Johns Hopkins University School of Medecine, "Mortality Analyses," 2021, https://coronavirus.jhu.edu/data/mortality.

Multinationalism in the Spanish Territorial Debate during the COVID-19 Crisis. The Case of Catalonia and Intergovernmental Relations

Marc Sanjaume-Calvet (iD) and Mireia Grau Creus

ABSTRACT

This paper analyses the relationship between the COVID-19 crisis and multinationalism in Spain from two complementary angles. First, it provides an overview on how the multinational and decentralized character of Spanish territorial politics shapes the response to the crisis. We find that the management of the crisis reflects and exacerbates the main features of the Spanish territorial model as a case of incomplete federalism with severe intergovernmental deficits. Second, we analyze the effects of the pandemic on Catalan self-determination demands through a brief description of parties, public opinion and governmental reactions. We argue that Catalan secessionism faces several new impediments as a result of the pandemic, but we also find that the COVID-19 crisis provides a window of opportunity for this movement regarding grievance-building and regional governmental performance and salience. We conclude with a general reflection on the ambivalent impact of COVID-19 crisis on Spanish regionalism and territorial politics. Overall, the COVID-19 crisis does not seem to mean an improvement but a potential setback for the accommodation of national diversity.

Introduction

"This virus does not respect borders."[1] These words, from the WHO director general, Tedros Adhanom Ghebreyesus, were the standard argument to justify the centralization of crisis management during the first steps of the pandemic in Spain. The state of alarm, declared on 14 March 2020 without consulting regional governments, imposed a unique commandment in Madrid on regional governments.[2] This first over-centralization reaction lasted for more than four months, renewing long-standing concerns about the Spanish territorial division of powers. The lockdown de-escalation phase was gradually accompanied by a reverse approach; during this phase, regional powers began to matter to the containment of the virus, and intergovernmental relations gained prominence. The territorial politics of pandemic management in Spain reflects both institutional features and territorial conflicts related to the heterogeneity of ideological and national identities of the country. How has the COVID-19 crisis been shaped by multinationalism in the Spanish case? Can we assess its impact on Spanish territorial politics? Has the COVID-19 crisis affected the Catalan territorial conflict?

The aim of this article is to answer these questions through an analysis of institutional actors during the first period of the pandemic, specifically the first wave and the beginning of the second in Spain and Catalonia (that is, from March 2020 to October

2020).[3] Our main argument is that the COVID-19 crisis may have an impact on Spanish territorial politics due to its capacity to deepen the deficits of the Spanish decentralization system, such as its underdeveloped system of intergovernmental relations. Moreover, the COVID-19 crisis, at least in the short term, has had a negative effect on the resolution of the Catalan territorial conflict (the major challenge to Spanish constitutional stability since 1978) because it has altered the political agenda and its priorities. As a result, political talks on the future of the region have been dropped. In this context, the window of opportunity for partisan polarization has been enlarged substantially and it has considerably narrowed that for making concessions and for seeking negotiations.

The article is structured as follows. First, we briefly summarize the emerging literature on federalism and nationalism related to crisis and COVID-19 management. Second, we describe how the Spanish territorial model has shaped the response to the crisis. Third, we analyze the impact of the COVID-19 crisis on the Catalan territorial conflict. We focus on institutional actors and public opinion and describe the main reactions to the Spanish Government management to the crisis, as well as the internal evolution of the pro-independence movement. Finally, we discuss our findings and their general implications.

Literature and theory

The COVID-19 crisis has created a boom of all kinds of social sciences academic production. Journal articles, blog posts, and books have bloomed, aiming at analyzing the pandemic's impacts on social and political life.[4] Nonetheless, the implications of this crisis for federal systems and multinationalism are still largely unknown. In this article, we bring together literature on federalism and nationalism to analyze the Spanish case. This section summarizes the evidence we have so far on the relationship between COVID-19 and these concepts found in the recent research.

The so-called "cavalry imaginary," borrowed from the American context, is common during times of emergency in all federal systems.[5] Centralization, single leadership, and eventually federal troops on terrain appear as common-sense solutions to human disasters both at practical and theoretical levels. At first glance, the efficiency principle seems to demand a unique commandment of the crisis. Historical and contemporary evidence suggests that crises and disasters generally stimulate the appetite of federal governments for the centralization of policy measures. While the two World Wars are classic examples of this centralizing tendency,[6] we can also find recent evidence, such as Hurricane Katrina or the September 11 terrorist attacks in the United States.[7] In addition, federal systems provide a unique institutional setting for political actors to manipulate responsibilities and dilute accountability.[8] Elites and institutions can use multilevel governance as a tool for blame-game strategies. In a study on the consequences of Hurricane Katrina, Maestas et al. concluded that "this phenomenon of muddied responsibility works equally well across levels of government (from federal to state). When blame can be shifted, elite actors will manipulate the stories to alter citizen responsibility judgments. Citizens respond to this manipulation, especially those who are predisposed to accept the alterative judgment, and shift blame accordingly."[9]

Recent contributions have already discussed this point regarding the COVID-19 crisis.[10] In an analysis on the US federal system performance during the pandemic, Carter and May[11] conclude that "the pandemic response reflects a feeble policy regime, reflected in inferior federal direction and an inconsistent, disorganized patchwork of state, local, and nongovernmental actions." According to Palermo,[12] even if initial reactions to the crisis suggest emergency powers and centralization as reasonable responses, federalism shows its strengths in managing the crisis because of its potential coordination, efficiency and specific policies tailored to local necessities. Buthe et al.,[13] in a study comparing unitary and federal democracies, found evidence that federal systems offer better heterogeneous regional responses to the virus, although they also observe in the Italian case that autonomy within a unitary system might be used for other (political) purposes than fighting the virus. Therefore, according to the literature, severe crises generally imply centralization trends, but heterogeneous policies are possible although they open the door to other political uses and do not guarantee more efficiency in fighting the pandemic. As in the US example, federalism might be used by political actors as a tool for deepening political polarization.[14]

Federalism and nationalism tend to be interlinked phenomena. Many federations are multinational and experience territorial tensions due to their internal diversity.[15] The literature on nationalism and COVID-19 suggests an expected effect of reinforcement of this political phenomenon, a global trend that was already there before the pandemic "shock" and implies the rise of exclusionary politics.[16] The crisis could have implied at least two complementary effects. First, the return of the state in the middle of the "deglobalization" process.[17] The pandemic could potentially accelerate this return as it can promote the emergence of populist and protectionist policies facing scarce medical resources and social or/and economic effects of the virus.[18] This might be fueled by the return of strong state nationalism, but it might entail a reinforcement of sub-state nationalisms and ethnic divisions as well.[19]

Second, there is evidence of a "rally around the flag" effect in the reaction to the crisis. This effect might entail stronger national sentiments, but it can provide additional popular support to institutions and even benefit incumbent political leaders or/and institutions not related to the pandemic management. In fact, rally effects were already observed in Denmark and other countries during the first months of the pandemic.[20]

Finally, there is little evidence on the effects on autonomy or self-determination demands of this crisis. Indigenous peoples' demands have obviously linked the fight against COVID-19 to territorial self-determination due to their situation of communitarian vulnerability regarding the virus.[21] Other authors suggest a general trend of counter-secessionist politics linked to the pandemic, at least when comparing Western European cases.[22]

Our specific framework of analysis for the Catalan case is inspired by the literature on secessionism[23] and social movements dynamics.[24] According to the literature, secessionist movements operate in a specific strategic field. Their main task is to make their home state accede to their demands, and alternatively, call the attention of the international community. However, as with any other political and social factors, they might face oscillating dynamics depending on incentives, critical junctures and windows of opportunity.[25] Obviously, these dynamics, including the windows of opportunity and repertory of action might be affected by the pandemic situation, as we will see.

In short, we expect to find a negative impact of COVID-19 pandemic on multinational accommodation in Spain and Catalonia. Our hypothesis is that the COVID-19 pandemic and its management could imply an increase in territorial tensions and national divides through the mechanisms described in this section: (a) A wave of state nationalism and return of (central state) in a regionalized (but not federal) territorial model (see below); (b) a "rally around the flag" effect both at state and sub-state levels implying more partisan polarization at various levels; and (c) a reinforcement of counter-secessionist policies during the pandemic and political fragmentation at sub-state level.

Multinationalism and COVID-19 in Spain

When on 14 March 2020 the Spanish Government declared the state of alarm to the whole territory and subsequently defined the institutional structures and decision-making bodies that would deal with the emergency, no other option apart from a centralized single commandment headed by the Spanish Ministry of Health seemed to be even thinkable. No consideration was paid to the autonomous communities within this emergency decision-making framework. Not even when, from a logistical perspective, executive powers on health are a responsibility of the autonomous Communities, and, from an analytical perspective, the idea that Spain is one of the most decentralized political systems in the world has been accepted and promoted from Spanish political parties and their respective think tanks.[26] In this sense, and following the path of reactions to catastrophes mentioned in the previous section, the initial impact of the unexpected COVID-19 crisis on the Spanish institutional setting exposed the fact that political decentralization is trapped in a mentally and institutionally centralizing frame.

The Kingdom of Spain is formally established as a uni-national state and does not recognize the existence of other nations but only of "nationalities," a term that remains undefined in constitutional texts. Constitutional case-law does not accept regional "national definitions" to have any political or legal consequence. In fact, nationalities and regions enjoy few veto powers.[27] The *Estado de las Autonomías* has both federal and unitary characteristics.[28] On the one hand, there are two levels of government, with regional governments and parliaments, regional competences and taxes, a territorial upper chamber (the Senate) and intergovernmental relations. On the other hand, however, regional powers are not constituent powers but rather the product of decentralization (they do not appear in the Constitution as such); the Senate, despite its "territorial" constitutional label, is a classical second parliamentary chamber that represents state-wide party lines on the basis of provinces (not ACs); the power distribution is biased toward central powers and regions do not have fiscal autonomy. In addition, shared rule in Spain is very weak compared to federal countries. Moreover, intergovernmental relations (IGR) remain basically vertical, controlled by the Spanish Government Ministers and underdeveloped. The IGR system lacks any principle of collaboration or loyalty.[29]

From the very beginning, the COVID-19 pandemic made clear that there is no articulation of shared-rule and that the already existing system of intergovernmental relations was, as a matter of fact, a policy system that relies on a hierarchically constitutional and legal framework with the Spanish Government and its administration in a paramount position. Therefore, the initial centralizing response could hardly have been otherwise. In need of an immediate and urgent reaction to an unexpected situation, responses to the health emergency could only be based upon "what you already are."[30] "What Spain already is" is a political system in which decentralization is framed into, and therefore constrained and limited by, a classical uni-national institutional setting.[31]

The COVID-19 crisis, thus, indicated that the evident absence of shared-rule is not just a simple deficit or inefficiency of the intergovernmental institutional setting; it is, rather, a question of state-wide institutional design and framing. Integrating the autonomous communities into Spanish-wide decision and policy-making processes cannot be reduced to creating new and more intergovernmental forums and on changing their internal proceedings, as it had been the policy path followed so far.[32] Neither would such integration depend on institutional evolution, as some views on the Spanish system have implicitly suggested, as institutions do not evolve "naturally," and more decentralization does not always imply more federalism.[33] The question is, rather, that the uni-national paradigm has shaped an institutional setting that blocks by default the promotion and, especially, the legitimacy of territorial voices within state-wide decision-making processes. It is, thus, more of a question of legitimacy than it is of internal institutional design.

In this sense, the political and administrative rationales (absence of shared-rule and uni-nationalism) framing a single commandment that excluded the autonomous communities of having any other role than that of being the executors, were linked to, at least, two aspects: the default-institutional setting, as said before, and the inexperience of political actors working through an efficient intergovernmentalist scheme. As for the first aspect, the constitutional and legal setting defining and articulating the three different types of exceptionality (state of alarm, state of exception and state of siege),[34] was neither approved nor subsequently adapted to match a decentralized political system in which shared-rule could ever be developed and which involved self-rule as a basis of the system. The central vertex of declaring and implementing any of the three states of exceptionality lies with the Spanish Government, that holds on its own the initiative, and the Congress (the Senate has no role at all), that authorizes extensions (state of alarm) and proposals. Of course, this is far from surprising, but it influenced how the immediate response to the crisis was framed: as the triggering of all constitutional and legal mechanisms does not involve the autonomous communities at all, any willingness to make them part of it could only emerge from a previous definition of this exclusion as a political problem.

As for the second aspect—inexperience—Spain, as with many other European countries, had no experience in managing large-scale catastrophes and/or health crises. This lack of experience had a double effect on framing the response: as the COVID-19 outbreak spread, with no available proven know-how, the system was not only inexperienced and unprepared in relation to the management of the pandemic itself (using Capano's terms for the Italian case[35]), but also in relation to the management of a pandemic as a decentralized political system.

The implications of the pandemic shape an analytical perspective of a double nature. On the one hand, testing the capacity to react to the crisis; and, on the other hand, unveiling that the system was unfit to adapt to the high level of decentralization in times of crisis. Thus, this situation revealed new aspects of the territorial system: either it was not as highly decentralized as it was supposed to be, and/or the analysis of the model emphasized for decades an optimistic perspective regarding intergovernmental cooperation.

The unique commandment led by the Spanish Government found itself facing logistical and political dilemmas: the exclusion of the autonomous communities from the decision-making processes on the management of the COVID-19 crisis came along with the recentralization of their powers on health to avoid policy diversity across the country. At the same time, the Spanish Government reinforced its message on the need to cooperate, although from its top-down perspective. Recentralizing in order to homogenize policy definitions and policy instruments clashed with the fact that the operative dimension of the health system was in the hands of the autonomous communities, so the dilemma appeared in terms of efficiency: deciding without having a clear picture of the implementation instruments was a clear handicap. In this sense, therefore, logistics brought about a timid questioning of the adequacy of the response. Nonetheless, the decisive factor that pushed for a change was the double political dilemma the Spanish Government had to face. As the extensions of the state of alarm were approved one after another by the Congress, the perception that the Spanish Government's idea of cooperation did not include any bottom-up participation at all started to spread. This stance was criticized by autonomous-community premiers from all political perspectives. In this sense, criticisms coming from all parties and the need to look for parliamentary support on other issues beyond the pandemic (the Spanish Government is a minority coalition government[36]), pushed the Spanish Government to re-address its approach to cooperation, opening the door to some participation of the ACs in the decision-making processes on the COVID-19 crisis. Participation consisted in changing the dynamics of the weekly meetings between the Prime Minister and the autonomous-community premiers from pure one-way communication meetings to meetings intended to define and agree on common criteria and measures. This new trend persisted during the de-escalation and the second wave of the pandemic since October 2020.

From a comparative perspective, the Spanish territorial reaction to the first wave of the pandemic was almost unique. In federal countries such as Germany, Belgium, Canada and Australia, pandemic measures were implemented which preserved sub-unit powers and reinforced intergovernmental relations (Canada, Germany) or shared-rule (Australia). Rozell and Wilcox[37] show that these countries benefited from their institutional setting and shared responsibilities between federal and states governments. Obviously, the territorial politics of the pandemic were not free of contention. The US case, partly due to party polarization, has not been an example of efficacy fighting the pandemic, but at the same time, federal powers were not overridden. The most similar case to the Spanish territorial centralization and political debates was Italy. In the Italian regionalized system, centralization was also imposed from the center although without a constitutional mandate, only through central legislation, and regions such as Lombardy raised their voice against the Spanish Government as in the Catalan case.[38]

To sum up, the impact of the pandemic on the Spanish decentralized system and multinational reality has mainly had to do with throwing light into its defining features.

The initial response was shaped by the institutional policy legacy: centralization and, consequently, the exclusion of the autonomous communities from the decision-making process. The change experienced since May 2020 by integrating the autonomous communities in some partial aspects of the COVID-19 crisis decision-making can be seen either as a first step toward a change in the conceptual framing of the system, or as an adaptative strategy meant to avoid both disagreements in the parliamentary arenas and part of the blaming for the rather chaotical management crisis. Time will tell whether the claims for homogenizing some indicators and for strengthening the Ministry of Health with "more resources" will not imply another drain of powers from the autonomous communities.[39]

The context of the pandemic: Catalan self-determination movement

Since the Catalan autonomous community has recently been actively demanding national recognition, self-determination, and secession we focus on the relationship between the pandemic situation, multinationalism, and this specific case. Indeed, the events of October 2017 can be seen from this perspective. Catalan authorities organized a unilateral referendum without a legal basis, mainly to compel the Spanish authorities to accept their self-determination demands. Moreover, the internal competition within the secessionist movement to achieve the secessionist goal as fast as possible implied a competition rationality explained by Qvortrup[40] as a competition proximity model[41] and it was the result of a long period of growing mobilization of the pro-independence political movement in Catalonia.

Since the October 2017 events and the subsequent suspension of Catalan autonomy, Catalan politics have been stuck in a frozen territorial conflict with Spanish authorities. Support for independence is now regarded as a deep change compared to traditional supports for incremental autonomy among Catalan public opinion.[42] Alternative territorial arrangements (federalism and regionalism) maintain high levels of support, those opposed to independence do not articulate an alternative project beyond status quo.

The Catalan political context, even before the coronavirus crisis, was already precarious regarding the self-determination movement and its objectives. In fact, the virus irrupted into Catalan politics in a moment of extreme uncertainty regarding the future of the movement. In fact, the consequences of the events of October 2017 still loom large in Catalonia far beyond the suspension. The prosecution and conviction of Catalan leaders, together with a myriad of other judicial proceedings against individuals, civil servants and senior officers are factors that have shaped strongly the political and social mood. This context conditioned at least three aspects of Catalan politics: regional authority, pro-secession political parties, and public opinion.

In January 2020, the Catalan Prime Minister (CPM), Joaquim Torra, announced that, once the annual budget was approved, he would call for early elections although he did not mention any specific date. In March 2020, both autonomous-community governmental officials and citizens were clearly aware that the term in office was over. However, there was still a pending issue: the date of the elections, given that the regional budget had to be approved first. The elections were finally called for February

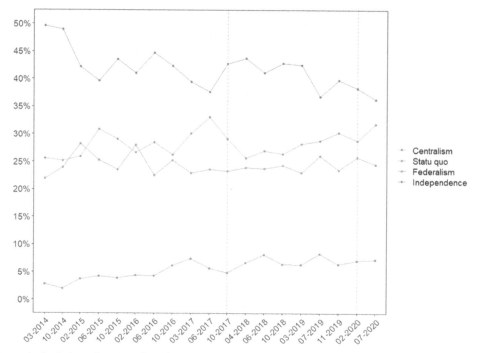

Figure 1. Evolution of territorial preferences in Catalonia (2014–2020).

2021, but the first steps of the fight against the pandemic had to be managed in a precarious political equilibrium within the regional minority coalition cabinet.

Mistrust between governmental partners (Junts per Catalunya—JxC—and Esquerra Republicana de Catalunya—ERC) became evident in many political decisions. The governmental debates between the members of the coalition on the pandemic management mixed with strategic divergences. In the early steps of the pandemic, the CPM (JxC) personally appointed epidemiology experts, undermining the powers of the regional Minister of Health, Alba Vergés (ERC). Later, coordination and participation in intergovernmental multilateral forums became an object of political disputes among coalition members as well. Governmental tensions were, to some extent, a reflect of strategic divergence and intra-party disagreements. Since 2017, the strategic unity among pro-independence actors that dominated the period 2012–2017, vanished and divergence regarding the future of the movement emerged (see Figure 1). This is not surprising since every political movement faces oscillations. In this case, a critical source of divergence came in June 2018 with the change of the state-wide political scenario: the successful motion of no confidence against Mariano Rajoy (PP) and the subsequent investiture of Pedro Sánchez (PSOE) as the Spanish Prime Minister (PM), opened the door to official talks on Catalonia's future, changing the strict "law and order" approach of the former conservative government. Within the Catalan pro-independence movement, there was a clear divergence on how to deal with the new scenario.[43]

Divergence has grown between hard-line secessionists who claim the legitimacy and mandate for secession of the 2017 unilateral independence referendum (most of the JxC leaders), and moderate secessionists (the mainstream position within ERC) who advocate for seizing the opportunity this new scenario has opened and push for a nego-tiated settlement with central powers. Moreover, after the "second round" of the 2019 General Elections, the thirteen ERC members of Congress abstained in the investiture voting contributing to the election of Pedro Sanchez as Prime Minister, together with the other regionalist parties and Podemos. The JxC parliamentary members, together with the members of Catalan radical left and pro-secession party, CUP, voted against, as did the three state-wide parties PP, Vox and Cs and other regionalist forces. The gen-eral strategic divergence ended up dividing the political space of JxC in a heated debate on its future. Under the leadership of the former CPM, Carles Puigdemont, JxC trans-formed from an electoral platform into a full-fledged secessionist political party.

As shown in Figure 1, the pro-secessionist government has faced the COVID-19 pan-demic in a context of relatively less enthusiasm for independence, although the holding of an official referendum on the future of the region as a potential solution to the terri-torial conflict remains a strong preference among Catalans. The pandemic seems to have reinforced supports for the *status quo* rather than for secession; however, we do not have enough data to statistically confirm this effect. In any case, this effect contrasts with what is observed in Scotland. In the post-Brexit Scottish case, the pandemic seems to reinforce support for independence. However, apart from noticing the contrast, no more can be said. Further research should be carried out in order to adequately com-pare whether the pandemic has had an impact on pro-secessionist supports in both cases.

COVID-19 and Catalan secessionism

The impact of the Covid-19 crisis on the Catalan self-determination movement has been Janus-faced, implying both obstacles and opportunities. In this section, we analyze the main factors affecting the self-determination objectives of the Catalan regional gov-ernment, parties, and civil society movement. First, we describe the context in which the COVID-19 crisis irrupted into Catalan politics. Second, following the literature on social movements, we analyze the main effects on its repertory of collective mobiliza-tion. Third, we identify windows of opportunity the crisis has opened. Finally, we search for provisional conclusions on the potential effects on the pro-independence polit-ical chessboard.

Effects on the repertory of collective action and strategic field of Catalan secessionism

The effects of the COVID-19 pandemic on the self-determination movement range from logistic to substantive aspects. First, as with any other political movement, nation-alist parties and organizations were forced to adapt their political activity to the pan-demic lockdown and other requirements. This has had, so far, at least two serious implications for the pro-independence forces. First, it has meant a more complex rela-tionship between leaders and party members in a context that already was logistically demanding, with their party leaders in jail after being sentenced to several years.[44] The pandemic measures have further restricted communication between the jailed leaders and the party, reducing their capacity to coordinate the strategies. Being in prison has also obviously cut their opportunities of public exposure. Before the COVID-19 crisis, the convicted secessionist leaders had been gradually granted some temporary release measures, but the Spanish Supreme Court overturned them using the pandemic as justification. This situation has obviously worsened political coordination. Second, lockdown and social distancing measures have affected the mobilization capacity of the movement. Popular mobilization on the streets has always been a powerful tool of the Catalan self-determination movement. Since the start of the pandemic, massive gatherings have been substituted by decentralized mobilizations that have had a limited media impact. The National Day of Catalonia, which had registered massive mobilizations over the last few years, could not gather independence supporters in Barcelona, and it provoked internal debates on the safety of these events. Reactive mobilizations were also scarce. In October 2020, the arrests of several pro-independence supporters accused of financing Puigdemont's network abroad, were criticized in the media but again could not be challenged on the streets.

From a more substantive perspective, the pandemic does not seem to provide an appropriate framework for rebuilding the self-determination roadmap. The context described in the previous paragraphs is unlikely to foster any long-term project on independence. The absence of pressure from grassroots militants on the streets, more radical than the average voters, and the urgence of fighting the pandemic contributed to maintain the self-determination movement in a long strategic stand-by.

The pandemic has first and foremost meant uncertainty regarding the political future. In these circumstances, public opinion seems to be more cautious and less enthusiastic than it was in relation to pro-independence plans. The ANC (National Assembly of Catalonia), a civil society pro-independence organization, insisted in March 2020 on the necessity of adopting a new Unilateral Declaration of Independence (UDI) if pro-independence parties reached more than 50% of the vote in the next regional elections; however, one must consider that this proposal, made in its general assembly, was held precisely during the initial moments of the pandemic. Later, in October, the ANC adopted a plan to monitor pro-independence party manifestos. However, the absence of any possible leverage for popular mobilization makes these resolutions minimally effective in influencing secessionist political parties and government.

However, despite the organizational and communication hurdles, some aspects of the pandemic could be a new window of opportunity regarding the management and territorial politics of the pandemic and for the self-determination movement. We turn to this point in the next subsection.

A window of opportunity?

The management of the pandemic has provided a window of opportunity for the secessionist perspective in three dimensions: grievance, performance, and salience.

The first steps of the pandemic management were criticized by the Catalan Government because of the centralization of regional powers. The literature on secessionism has well established the relevance of economic and political grievances in constructing secessionist movements.[45] In this sense, the PSOE-Podemos coalition government provided a powerful grievance to the secessionist narrative that, later, would be adopted by other territories, such as the Madrid region. In the Catalan political context, the immediate centralization of powers and declaration of State of Alarm was identified as an attack on Catalan self-government. Health, after all, is a matter under the powers of the Catalan administration. In general terms, two common criticisms came from the autonomous communities regarding the immediate centralization of powers: the first was that centralization would negatively affect efficiency in fighting the pandemic; the second was that centralization lacked or had little legitimacy. Moreover, the Catalan Government also criticized the centralization of lockdown decisions, decisions on sanitary measures and even the centralization of purchase of sanitary material such as masks. From its very beginning, the narrative behind these grievances was clear: an independent Catalonia would perform much better in fighting the COVID-19 crisis. In a radio interview, the Catalan government spokesperson was asked what an independent Catalan government would have done and stated "I'm sure there wouldn't have been so many dead or so many infected and this pandemic could probably have been controlled in a different way."[46]

During the first weeks of the State of Alarm (14–29 March 2020), the Catalan Government complained to the Spanish Government about what it considered a soft lockdown (the economy was still functioning) and asked for stronger measures against the pandemic such as a "total lockdown" that could only be triggered and implemented by the Spanish Government, which is what finally happened on 29 March 2020. The State of Alarm was then extended until 10 May when the de-escalation phase began. Again, during de-escalation, many grievances against centralization were raised, but this time designed to criticize the de-escalation phases and the necessity of adapting the de-escalation speed to the Catalan territorial necessities. In short, the centralization of lockdown and health measures offered a good opportunity for grievance-building rhetoric, which is central to any self-determination movement.

However, grievances from the Catalan governmental coalition, supported by other regional authorities such as the Basque Government, did not show unity of action within the framework of Spanish institutions. Table 1 tracks the votes for extending the State of Alarm decree during the first and second waves of the pandemic (a compulsory vote every 15 days according to the Spanish Constitution). The votes show a more nuanced picture compared to the relative unity shown by the governing coalition partners in Catalonia vis-a-vis the Spanish Government. ERC abstained in the first vote and maintained it up to the fourth extension; JxC abstained in the first and second extension but switched to "No" already in the third. In the sixth vote, as the expected result

Table 1. State of Alarm COVID-19 crisis extension votes in Spanish Congress (2020).

	1st wave						2nd wave
	1st	2nd	3rd	4th	5th	6th	1st
	25th March	9th April	26 April	10th May	24th May	7th June	29th October
ERC	Abst	Abst	Abst	No	No	Abst	Yes
Junts	Abst	Abst	No	No	No	No	No/Abst[a]
CUP	Abst	No	No	No	No	No	Abst
Yes/No (Abst.)	321/0 (28)	270/54 (25)	269/60 (16)	178/75 (97)	177/162 (11)	177/155 (18)	194/53 (99)

[a]Deputies belonging to "Junts" platform split votes due to party-line differences.
Own elaboration on official data at *Congreso de los Diputados* database, available at: http://congreso.es

was rather unclear, ERC stepped back to abstention to facilitate the approval. The extension votes of the second wave (voted on 25 October) reflected even more the strategic divergences between the two parties as their votes went into completely opposite directions: ERC voted in favor; JxC voted against. The internal cohesion of the JxC parliamentary group split as members voted differently following the alignment criteria of each internal political family. The total support to the State of Alarm extensions shown in Table 1 reflects the difficulties of the Spanish minority coalition government to obtain parliamentary supports to legitimize the State of Alarm. The heterogeneous parliamentary support that invested Pedro Sanchez (leftist and regional parties) was extremely fragile from the very beginning of the term and, therefore, forced PSOE to find new parliamentary alliances. This need for stable and permanent support became even more urgent in March 2020. During the pandemic, the PSOE-Podemos coalition have been facing a fierce opposition from PP and radical-right Vox. The latter has organized rallies against the Spanish Government's management of pandemic all over the country. In September 2020, Vox tabled a strategic motion of no-confidence that was only supported by their own 52 members. In short, the pandemic situation puts more pressure on the Spanish Government and, during the first votes of the State of Alarm, distanced the PSOE-Podemos governmental coalition from its support among pro-independence parties; this support was then replaced by Ciudadanos. Spanish government's legitimacy was affected by a strong centralization without homogeneous territorial and political supports.

The performance of the autonomous-community governments became more relevant during the de-escalation phase. Although performance is a goal pursued by all parties once in government, secessionist parties often struggle to appear as effective in managing government affairs at a regional level, and simultaneously "radical" enough in their secessionist objectives.[47] After a long "grievance" period of centrally controlled lockdown, the autonomous-community governments recovered their powers in June 2020 and began to have effective command of pandemic management. This new scenario was a challenge and a sort of reversal in the blame-game of pandemic management. In July 2020, a solid increase of COVID-19 cases in Catalonia was used to blame Catalan authorities of mismanaging the crisis when, at the same time, these authorities were blaming the Spanish Government. On this blame-game issue, public opinion seems to be divided following, precisely, political lines.

As we show in Figure 2, using data collected in October 2020, we observe that many pro-independence voters supported the grievance discourse regarding Catalan management of the crisis: "This Government knows how to solve the problems of the pandemic, but it needs more powers and more resources," while this is not the case of centralist or federalist voters. Unsurprisingly, these positions reversed when responding to the Spanish Government.

We do not observe many differences before and after the COVID-19 crisis in terms of governmental evaluation. As we show in Figure 3, governmental evaluation seems to improve as a general trend after the pandemic outbreak, although there is no statistical significance. Surprisingly, preferences for the status quo seem to be linked to positive evaluations on the Catalan Government, while, to a certain extent, people expressing their preferences for centralization and people supporting federalism seem to shyly

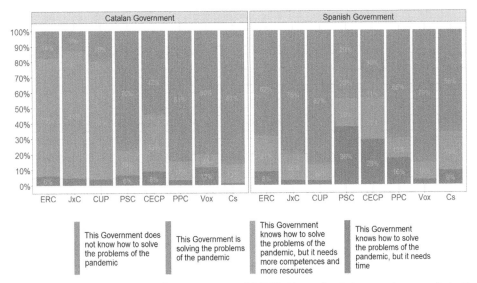

Figure 2. Opinion on governmental management of COVID-19 pandemic by vote in general elections.

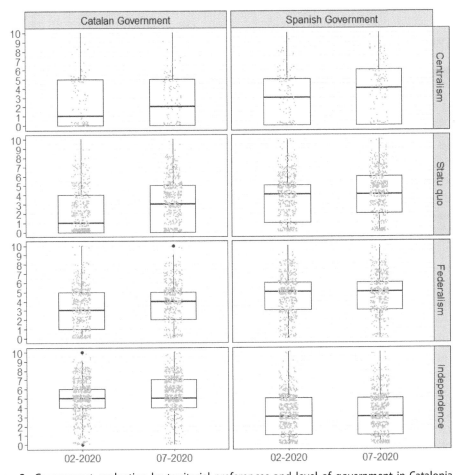

Figure 3. Government evaluation by territorial preferences and level of government in Catalonia.

show some good impression on the management of the crisis by the Catalan Government. In contrast, only those who express their preferences for centralization and status quo, have a good impression of the Spanish government capacity of managing the crisis. This could imply more margin of maneuver for an intergovernmental management of the pandemic (as we observe during the second wave of the virus) and less room for grievances against the Spanish Government.

Finally, "governmental salience" has been a crucial dimension in shaping the window of opportunity provided by the pandemic. We do not have data on salience, but it seems clear that the Catalan authorities, having much more leeway to implement their own policy, are more concerned by this new salience regarding the pandemic. An example of this trend was the appointment of an expert with a very technical profile, Dr. Josep Maria Argimon, as Health Secretary of the Catalan Government. Argimon also has the key role of officially communicating all new measures decided by the Catalan Government. In this second declaration of the State of Alarm, the autonomous-community governments oversee the pandemic, although the Spanish Government sets the range in which regional variations of the measures are allowed. In this sense, for instance, in relation to curfews, the Spanish authorities established that it cannot start before 10 pm and no later than midnight, and that it cannot end before 5 am and after 7 am. The Catalan Government adopted a long nocturnal curfew from 10 pm to 6am and a strict local (perimetral) lockdown on weekends (30 October 2020).

A balance of the pro-independence political chessboard

At the time of this writing, the second wave of COVID-19 has just started and it is still too early to assess the long-term impact of the crisis on the political chessboard. Based on this brief analysis of the first seven months of the pandemic, we consider that some logistic and substantive elements hinder self-determination goals in pandemic times, but at the same time recognize this crisis might be regarded as a window of opportunity. Which actors gain and which ones lose because of the pandemic crisis in the Catalan territorial conflict?

An initial analysis seems to suggest a potential polarization effect in the short term that would be cooled down by the salience of sub-state governance and a certain moderation of public opinion. When comparing with the political situation just before the outbreak of the virus, it seems that the pandemic has broadened the gap between the two sides of the conflict. On the one hand, the Spanish Government seems to be now less prone to political alliances with the Catalan parties in government as the crisis has provided clear incentives to accept supports from the center-liberal party Ciudadanos. Moreover, the crisis has stimulated Vox[48] and, to a lesser extent, some PP autonomous-community leaders to put pressure onto the Spanish Government, while some Socialist territorial leaders have openly criticized the management of the crisis. On the other hand, grievances against the Spanish Government and its new alliance with Ciudadanos, seem to have fueled more radical positions within the pro-independence movement. In one of his last interviews as CPM, Joaquim Torra described the existing Catalan self-government as "an obstacle to achieve the independence."[49] However, as we have described in the previous subsection, governmental performance and salience are now more crucial than ever. Therefore, the general perceptions indicate that there is less room for grievances against the Spanish Government, and more appetite for regional government performance.

In the Spanish PM investiture debate in January 2020, ERC abstained in return for a promise of starting official talks between the Spanish and the Catalan governments on the future of Catalonia.[50] Afterwards, a dialogue table with representatives from both governments was constituted but they met only once.[51] However, the start of the pandemic in mid-March blocked the situation and the dialogue table has, so far, not been called. In brief, the pandemic has affected this initial expectation of starting a negotiated process.

Discussion and conclusions: hard times for multinational accommodation

Our analysis of the relationship between multinationalism and COVID-19 in the case of Spain sheds light on the potential territorial effects of this crisis. Overall, the COVID-19 crisis has a relevant territorial dimension and affects multinationalism, in the sense of accommodating national diversity, and does not seem to mean an improvement but a potential setback for those pushing for sub-state nationalism. In the context of multinational states, the automatic institutional choice for centralization in fighting the pandemic could be understood as one indicator of the weakness of central governments' internal territorial legitimacy. On the one hand, we find evidence of deficits and destabilizing effects, such as party polarization implying more territorial tensions. On the other hand, we observe potential changes in the patterns of public policies to fight the pandemic that could led to a future more federal territorial approach; the indicator of this change lies on the fact that the decision-making process revolving around the COVID-19 measures, includes the autonomous communities.

The analysis from a territorial perspective of the crisis management in Spain confirms the already existing evidence about crisis and federalism. We observe a centralization trend, at least as a primary reaction following a sort of "cavalry imaginary" narrative. This reaction is also shaped by the nature of the Spanish territorial system. We subscribe to Capano's approach: "you can only be what you already are." In this sense, the Spanish reaction in March 2020 to the COVID-19 crisis completely unveiled its centralized and nonfederal nature, as well as its intergovernmental deficits. However, the subsequent events and political fragility of the governmental coalition led to a more open approach to territorial management. In this sense, it seems that there is some potential for intergovernmental coordination based on multilateral principles. In this new dynamic, we do not observe any multinational dimension. That is, we observe more decentralization, still controlled from Madrid, but not any multinational dynamic.

In fact, if we exclusively focus on multinationalism, the COVID-19 pandemic does not imply good news for the accommodation of national diversity in Spain for various reasons. Firstly, intergovernmental relations remain symmetrical among regions. As is usually the case, multinational perspectives, if any, are channeled through partisan negotiations in the *Congreso de los Diputados*. In this case, some Basque and Catalan parties (PNB, EH Bildu, ERC, Junts) have had a relevant role in shaping the de-escalation of the first wave and the measures of the second wave (from October 2020). At the end, these pressures have applied to all the autonomous communities without asymmetries within the decision-making powers in multilateral intergovernmental forums.[52] The only asymmetries are related to specific details such as curfew timings and minor restrictions. No multinational approach was even thought to be applied.

Secondly, political, and social tensions derived from the COVID-19 have empowered Vox, a far-right ultranationalist party, providing a window of opportunity to this radical form of Spanish nationalism. The strategic non-confidence motion tabled by this party is proof of this opportunity although the electoral benefits of such a move are still unknown. In any case, the strengthening of Vox's style of nationalism is not a positive sign for improving national diversity accommodation. Regarding political alliances, as explained in previous sections, the leftist coalition in the Spanish Government has attracted supports from Ciudadanos.

Thirdly, the Catalan self-determination movement has become more polarized, although the internal competition within the pro-independence movement already existed before the crisis. The effects of the COVID-19 crisis have worsened the relationships between the Spanish Government and the autonomous-community authorities by increasing territorial grievances and reinforcing those criticizing (JxC) the moderate approach of ERC. Moreover, the crisis has postponed the promised dialogue table on the Catalan conflict, and worsened some logistical aspects related to internal communication among secessionist leaders. In short, the pandemic has worsened the personal situation of the leaders in jail and in exile, while, at the same time, it has closed the potential institutional avenues of conflict resolution that were open in early 2020. The effects of the pandemic have polarized strategic positions between parties and reinforced hard-liners, making agreements on territorial issues less probable in the short term.

The Spanish case is a prototypical example of centralization facing an unexpected crisis[53] and nationalism exacerbation[54] involving an increase of territorial tension. In this article we find a negative relationship between the COVID-19 crisis and multinationalism. Fighting the pandemic in Spain has meant more centralization, an increase of Spanish nationalism, closing institutional avenues of territorial conflicts resolution and partisan polarization regarding political strategies. However, these findings may be temporary and might change in the future. Most of these effects were already present before the pandemic and their current trend might be contingent to the situation and imply few or null structural changes. In any case, our findings are consistent with previous research on federalism, nationalism, and COVID-19 crisis.

The implications of these findings are relevant for future research on the effects of COVID-19 pandemic and crisis in general. More in-depth research can shed light on the evolution of the reaction to the crisis, as well as its effects on public opinion and political actors. Recent developments of the Spanish policies to fight the pandemic suggest that a plural approach might be more effective than a centralized one. It also highlights the relevance of governmental performance and salience as a potential variable that might moderate nationalistic reactions to the crisis.[55] Viruses might not respect borders, but governmental jurisdictions, and accountability, seem to matter both for granting political stability and public opinion approval.

Notes

1. See https://www.bioworld.com/articles/433360-this-virus-does-not-respect-borders-says-who-director-general-but-containment-still-possible.
2. The state of alarm (*Estado de alarma*) is the lowest of the three levels of state of emergency foreseen in the Spanish Constitution (Art.116.2) and it can be declared (in all the territory or parts of it) in case of: serious risk, catastrophe or public calamity, health crises, situations of shortages of necessity products, paralysis of essential public services for the community among other reasons. It means limitation of movement or permanence of people or vehicles at certain times and places, temporary searches of all kinds of goods and imposition of civil conscription, intervention and temporary occupation of industries, factories, workshops, farms or locals of any nature, reporting it to the concerned Ministries, the use of services or the consumption of basic necessities may be limited or rationed, the necessary orders may be issued to ensure the supply of the markets and the performance of the affected services and production centers. See also https://english.elpais.com/politics/2020-03-22/spanish-government-to-extend-state-of-alarm-for-15-days.html
3. Specific data on the impact of Covid-19 can be found here: https://www.mscbs.gob.es/en/profesionales/saludPublica/ccayes/alertasActual/nCov/situacionActual.htm
4. See, for example, the number of publications on COVID-19, federalism and territorial politics retrieved here: https://www.mcgill.ca/federalism/federalism-covid-19-pandemic.
5. Thomas Birkland, and Sarah Waterman, "Is Federalism the Reason for Policy Failure in Hurricane Katrina?," *Publius: The Journal of Federalism* 38, no. 4 (2008): 692–714.
6. See for example on the Canadian case: André Lecours, "Dynamic De/Centralization in Canada," *Publius: The Journal of Federalism* 49, no. 1 (2019): 57–83.
7. Elizabeth F. Kent, "Where's the Cavalry - Federal Response to 21st Century Disasters Note," *Suffolk University Law Review* 40, no. 1 (2006): 181–214; Jason Scott Johnston, "Disasters and Decentralisation," *The Geneva Papers on Risk and Insurance - Issues and Practice* 37, no. 2 (2012): 228–56.
8. William M. Downs, "Accountability Payoffs in Federal Systems? Competing Logics and Evidence from Europe's Newest Federation," *Publius: The Journal of Federalism* 29, no. 1 (1999): 87–110.
9. C. D. Maestas, L. R. Atkeson, T. Croom, and L. A. Bryant, "Shifting the Blame: Federalism, Media, and Public Assignment of Blame following Hurricane Katrina," *Publius: The Journal of Federalism* 38, no. 4 (2008): 609–32, 627.
10. Daniel Béland, André Lecours, Mireille Paquet, and Trevor Tombe, "A Critical Juncture in Fiscal Federalism? Canada's Response to COVID-19," *Canadian Journal of Political Science* 53, no. 2 (2020): 239–5; Rebecca L. Haffajee, and Michelle M. Mello, "Thinking Globally, Acting Locally - The U.S. Response to Covid-19," *The New England Journal of Medicine* 382, no. 22 (2020): e75; Nancy J. Knauer, *The COVID-19 Pandemic and Federalism* (Rochester, NY: Social Science Research Network, 2020).
11. David P. Carter, and Peter J. May, "Making Sense of the U.S. COVID-19 Pandemic Response: A Policy Regime Perspective," *Administrative Theory & Praxis* 42, no. 2 (2020): 265–13.
12. Francesco Palermo, "Is There a Space for Federalism in Times of Emergency?," Verfassungsblog (blog), 2020, https://verfassungsblog.de/is-there-a-space-for-federalism-in-times-of-emergency/.
13. Tim Buthe, Joan Barceló, Cindy Cheng, Paula Ganga, Luca Messerschmidt, Allison Spencer Hartnett, and Robert Kubinec, *Patterns of Policy Responses to the COVID-19 Pandemic in Federal vs. Unitary European Democracies* (Rochester, NY: Social Science Research Network: 2020).
14. Mark J. Rozell, and Clyde Wilcox, "Federalism in a Time of Plague: How Federal Systems Cope with Pandemic," *The American Review of Public Administration* 50, no. 6–7 (2020): 519–25.

15. Ferran Requejo, *Democracy and National Pluralism* (London; New York: Routledge, 2001); Alain-G. Gagnon and Soeren Keil, *Understanding Federalism and Federation* (London; New York: Routledge, 2016).
16. Florian Bieber, "Global Nationalism in Times of the COVID-19 Pandemic," *Nationalities Papers* (2020): 1–13.
17. Aristotle Kallis, "Populism, Sovereigntism, and the Unlikely Re-Emergence of the Territorial Nation-State," *Fudan Journal of the Humanities and Social Sciences* 11, no. 3 (2018): 285–302.
18. See: https://www.project-syndicate.org/commentary/covid-19-deglobalization-pandemic-by-harold-james-2020-02?barrier=accesspaylog
19. Yael Tamir, *Why Nationalism* (Princeton: Princeton University Press, 2019).
20. Martin Baekgaard, Julian Christensen, Jonas Krogh Madsen, and Kim Sass Mikkelsen, "Rallying around the Flag in Times of COVID-19: Societal Lockdown and Trust in Democratic Institutions," *Journal of Behavioral Public Administration* 3, no. 2 (2020): 1–12.
21. Sacha McMeeking, Helen Leahy, and Catherine Savage, "An Indigenous Self-Determination Social Movement Response to COVID-19," *AlterNative: An International Journal of Indigenous Peoples* 16, no. 4 (2020): 395–8.
22. Jonathan Parker, "Assessing the Impact of Covid-19 on Independence Movements in Catalonia, Flanders and Scotland." *EUROPP* (blog), 2020, https://blogs.lse.ac.uk/europpblog/2020/06/22/assessing-the-impact-of-covid-19-on-independence-movements-in-catalonia-flanders-and-scotland/.
23. Ryan D. Griffiths, *Age of Secession* (Cambridge: Cambridge University Press, 2016); Ryan D. Griffiths, "Secessionist Strategy and Tactical Variation in the Pursuit of Independence," *Journal of Global Security Studies*, 6, no. 1 (2021): ogz082. doi:10.1093/jogss/ogz082. Ryan D. Griffiths and Diego Muro, *Strategies of Secession and Counter-Secession* (Colchester: ECPR Press, 2020); David S. Siroky, Sean Mueller, and Michael Hechter, "Center-Periphery Bargaining in the Age of Democracy," *Swiss Political Science Review* 22, no. 4 (2016): 439–53; Michae Hechter, *Containing Nationalism* (Oxford: Oxford University Press, 2000).
24. Sidney Tarrow, *Power in Movement: Social Movements and Contentious Politics* (Cambridge: Cambridge University Press, 1998); Charles Tilly, *Dynamics of Contention. Cambridge Studies in Contentious Politics* (Cambridge: Cambridge University Press, 2001).
25. Ibid.
26. See Pedro Sánchez, "España puede: recuperación, transformación y resiliencia," Madrid, 31 de agosto de 2020 (conference by Sánchez at Casa América, 2020); PSOE, 2013 Hacia una estructura federal del Estado, Declaració de Granada (6 July 2013); José Mª Aznar La Constitución de los españoles, Fundación Alternativas.
27. Pau Bossacoma Busquets and Marc Sanjaume-Calvet, "Asymmetry as a Device for Equal Recognition and Reasonable Accommodation of Majority and Minority Nations. A Country Study on Constitutional Asymmetry in Spain," in *Constitutional Asymmetry in Multinational Federalism: Managing Multinationalism in Multi-Tiered Systems*, edited by Patricia Popelier and Maja Sahadžić (Cham: Springer International Publishing, 2019), 429–60.
28. Eliseo Aja, *El estado autonómico: federalismo y hechos diferenciales* (Madrid: Alianza, 2003); Ferran Requejo, *Multinational Federalism and Value Pluralism: The Spanish Case* (London; New York: Routledge, 2005); Michael Burgess and Alain-G. Gagnon, eds., *Federal Democracies* (London; New York: Routledge, 2010); Luis Moreno, 2010. "Federal Democracy in Plural Spain," in *Federal Democracies*, edited by Michael Burgess and Alain-G. Gagnon (London; New York: Routledge, 2016), 160–77.
29. We provided a full explanation of the Spanish territorial system and the Catalan autonomy in this report published by the series World Autonomies project by EURAC: http://www.world-autonomies.info/tas/catalonia/Pages/default.aspx
30. Giliberto Capano, "Policy Design and State Capacity in the COVID-19 Emergency in Italy: If You Are Not Prepared for the (Un)Expected, You Can Be Only What You Already Are," *Policy and Society* 39, no. 3 (2020): 326–44.

31. Requejo, *Multinational Federalism and Value Pluralism.*
32. José María Pérez-Medina, "Dinámica de Las Conferencias Sectoriales. Entre la Intergubernamentalidad y la Cooperación Administrativa," *Revista D'estudis Autonòmics i Federals* 31, (2020): 17–64.
33. Mireia Grau Creus, "Checkmate to the Spanish Decentralization? The Decline of Public Support for Spain's Autonomous Communities," in *Identities, Trust, and Cohesion in Federal Systems: Public Perspectives*, edited by Jack Jedwab and John Kincaid (Montreal: McGill-Queen's Press – McGill-Queen's University Press, 2019), 57–84.
34. See Article 116 Spanish Constitution.
35. Capano, "Policy Design and State Capacity."
36. PSOE-Podemos with, respectively, 120 and 35 parliamentary members out of 350.
37. Rozell and Wilcox, "Federalism in a Time of Plague."
38. See Davide Vampa, "The Territorial Politics of Coronavirus: Is This the Hour of Central Government?," *Democratic Audit* (blog), 2020, http://eprints.lse.ac.uk/107870/. On the relationship between the pandemic and territorial politics also see the compendium of resources at McGill University website: https://www.mcgill.ca/federalism/federalism-covid-19-pandemic
39. See https://www.mscbs.gob.es/gabinete/notasPrensa.do?id=5022
40. Matt Qvortrup, *Referendums and Ethnic Conflict* (Philadelphia: University of Pennsylvania Press, 2014).
41. Jaume López and Marc Sanjaume-Calvet, "The Political Use of de Facto Referendums of Independence the Case of Catalonia," *Representation* 56, no. 4 (2020): 501–19; Marc Sanjaume-Calvet and Elvira Riera-Gil, "Languages, Secessionism and Party Competition in Catalonia: A Case of de-Ethnicising Outbidding?," *Party Politics* October (2020). doi:10.1177/1354068820960382
42. Xavier Cuadras-Morató, ed., *Catalonia: A New Independent State in Europe?: A Debate on Secession Within the European Union* (London; New York: Routledge, 2016); Ivan Serrano, "Just a Matter of Identity? Support for Independence in Catalonia," *Regional & Federal Studies* 23, no. 5 (2013): 523–45; López and Sanjaume-Calvet, "The Political Use of de Facto Referendums"; Toni Rodon, and Marc Guinjoan, "When the Context Matters: Identity, Secession and the Spatial Dimension in Catalonia," *Political Geography* 63 (2018): 75–87; Jordi Muñoz, and Raül Tormos, "Economic Expectations and Support for Secession in Catalonia: Between Causality and Rationalization," *European Political Science Review* 7, no. 2 (2015): 315–41.
43. Question: In any case, how do you think this relationship [between Catalonia and Spain] should be? Do you think that Catalonia should be? 1. A region of Spain; 2. An autonomous community of Spain (status quo); 3. A state in a federal Spain; 4. An independent State; 98. Does not know; 99. Does not answer.
44. This situation has repeatedly been denounced by Amnesty International, see: https://www.es.amnesty.org/en-que-estamos/noticias/noticia/articulo/espana-la-condena-por-sedicion-a-jordi-sanchez-y-jordi-cuixart-una-amenaza-a-los-derechos-a-la-liber/. United Nations Arbitrary Detention Working Group denounced the imprisonment of Catalan leaders during more than two years before the trial, see https://www.reuters.com/article/us-spain-un-catalonia-idUSKCN1SZ1YW
45. Brandon M. Boylan, "In Pursuit of Independence: The Political Economy of Catalonia's Secessionist Movement," *Nations and Nationalism* 21, no. 4 (2015): 761–85; Le Breton, and Michel Shlomo Weber, "The Art of Making Everybody Happy: How to Prevent a Secession," IMF Staff Papers 50, no. 3 (2003): 403–35; Siroky et al., "Center-Periphery Bargaining in the Age of Democracy"; David S. Siroky and John Cuffe, "Lost Autonomy, Nationalism and Separatism," *Comparative Political Studies* 48, no. 1 (2015): 3–34.
46. See https://www.lavanguardia.com/politica/20200420/48623821222/meritxell-budo-govern-independencia-coronavirus-muertos-infectados.html
47. Malcolm Harvey, and Peter Lynch, "Inside the National Conversation: The SNP Government and the Politics of Independence 2007-2010," *Scottish Affairs* 80 (First Series),

no. 1 (2012): 91–116; Robert Johns, James Mitchell, and Christopher J. Carman, "Constitution or Competence? The SNP's Re-Election in 2011," *Political Studies* 61, no. 1_suppl (2013): 158–78; Rob Johns and James Mitchell, *Takeover: Explaining the Extraordinary Rise of the SNP* (London: Biteback Publishing; 2016).

48. See BBC, "Coronavirus: Anti-lockdown car protest draws thousands," https://www.bbc.com/news/world-europe-52783936
49. See https://www.vilaweb.cat/noticies/quim-torra-hem-de-ser-conscients-que-aixo-no-pot-continuar-aixi/
50. See https://english.elpais.com/politics/catalonia_independence/2020-01-31/spanish-pm-backtracks-on-postponing-talks-with-catalan-government.html
51. See https://english.elpais.com/politics/catalonia_independence/2020-02-06/spanish-pm-meets-with-catalan-premier-ahead-of-talks-on-regions-future.html
52. Mainly the *Consejo Interterritorial del Sistema Nacional de Salud* (CISNS).
53. Knauer, *The COVID-19 Pandemic and Federalism*.
54. Bieber, "Global Nationalism in Times of the COVID-19 Pandemic."
55. César Colino, "Intergovernmental Relations in the Spanish Federal System: In Search of a Model," in *The Ways of Federalism in Western Countries and the Horizons of Territorial Autonomy in Spain*, edited by Alberto López-Basaguren and Leire Escajedo San Epifanio (Berlin Heidelberg: Springer, 2013), 111–24; Mireia Grau Creus, "Spain: Incomplete Federalism," in *Federalism and Political Performance*, edited by Ute Wachendorfer-Schmidt (London; New York: Routledge, 2000); Michael Hechter, "The Dynamics of Secession," *Acta Sociologica* 35, no. 4 (1992): 267–83; Ferran Requejo and Marc Sanjaume-Calvet, "Recognition and Political Accommodation: From Regionalism to Secessionism – The Catalan Case," in *Recognition and Redistribution in Multinational Federations*, edited by Jean-François Grégoire and Michael Jewkes (Leuven: Leuven University Press, 2015), 246

ORCID

Marc Sanjaume-Calvet iD http://orcid.org/0000-0001-8723-1618

OPEN ACCESS

Multinationalism, Constitutional Asymmetry and COVID: UK Responses to the Pandemic

Karlo Basta and Ailsa Henderson

ABSTRACT
This article explores how the asymmetric institutionalization of the United Kingdom's multinationality interacted with the COVID-19 pandemic. The UK's political elite has traditionally accepted the country's multinational character, but democratic institutionalization of it occurred relatively recently and in a remarkably asymmetric manner. Only the UK's minority nations possess devolved governments, while the largest nation, England, is governed directly from the center. This framework has consequences for the pandemic response. It has clarified the relevance of devolved legislatures, but also highlights continued resistance of the UK's governing elite to acknowledge the multi-level character of the state.

The United Kingdom is an unusual multinational state. Its legitimizing ideology—British unionism—acknowledges multinationality in ways that stand out from other such settings where state nationalism tends to crowd out national pluralism. At the same time, the UK's institutions constitute a singularly asymmetric expression of that multinationality. While the populations of Scotland, Wales, and Northern Ireland are governed both by the UK and devolved governments, the country's largest nation, England, is governed directly from the center, without a set of intermediate democratic institutions, offering incomplete coverage across England. Westminster, therefore, wears multiple hats, generating, at times, policy for the whole of the UK, for England and Wales, or for England alone.

The main reason behind this configuration is the way in which the UK's political elites, drawn predominantly from England, conceive of the state they are governing. Rather than seeing the 1998 Belfast Agreement and the 1999 devolution settlements as the central feature of the UK's constitutional DNA, the country's leaders regard them as issues to be managed on an ad hoc basis whenever a crisis emerges into open view in one of the devolved jurisdictions. By extension, the multi-level character of the state is not reflected in the decision-making processes at the center. Instead, the UK is run largely as a unitary state, with the governing elites frequently conflating the priorities of the largest constituent nation—England—with those of the entire country. This elite perspective is rooted in broad-based indifference among the English population to the United Kingdom's multinational character.[1]

This is an Open Access article distributed under the terms of the Creative Commons Attribution-NonCommercial-NoDerivatives License (http://creativecommons.org/licenses/by-nc-nd/4.0/), which permits non-commercial re-use, distribution, and reproduction in any medium, provided the original work is properly cited, and is not altered, transformed, or built upon in any way.

In this article, we show how the UK's peculiarly (under)institutionalized multinational, multi-level settlement interacted with the COVID-19 pandemic. In line with the focus of this special issue, we explore both how the UK's multinationality influenced the country's approach to the pandemic, and how the pandemic has reflected on the UK multinational settlement. On the one hand, we show that the rather weak institutionalization of the multi-level system has militated against close intergovernmental collaboration in response to the crisis. This system has also given the devolved governments the opportunity to *visibly* differentiate themselves from their UK counterpart. The pandemic seems to have reinforced centrifugal tendencies that were already intensifying in response to Brexit in Scotland and Wales, if from different starting points. On the other hand, the pandemic and the multiple crises (for example, health and economic/fiscal) it has generated have thrown into sharper relief the lack of awareness of, or attention to, the state's multi-level character among England-based political and media elites, a phenomenon we cover in the last substantive section.

We offer two caveats. First, since we foreground the role of the Anglo-British elites in shaping the politics of the UK's multinationality, and in light of space constraints, we do not explore in detail the impact of the pandemic on the internal politics of devolved jurisdictions. Such an examination would require an article of its own. We nevertheless touch upon some of the ways the pandemic has interacted with the politics of national identity in sub-state nations. We focus on Scotland in particular given majority support for independence in recent polls, support that predates the pandemic but that has interacted with it in interesting ways.[2] Second, in light of the thematic focus of this special issue, we endeavor to cover a lot of ground in relatively short space—including both the impact of the UK's multinational settlement on pandemic response and the influence of the pandemic on the UK's multinational context. We are aware that this necessitates a more limited treatment of both sets of issues, but we believe it is important to contextualize the interaction between multinationality and COVID-19 from both angles in order to provide readers with a more comprehensive image of the interaction between UK's multinationality and the pandemic.

In the next section, we point to typical characteristics of multinational states, including the kinds of ideational and institutional configurations that tend to arise in response to claims by minority nations. Our focus is on majority and minority national identities and narratives that tend to emerge, and the ways in which these narratives shape the political contestation at the heart of multinational states. In the second section, we contrast the UK multinational experience to this pattern and suggest how the ideational and institutional dimensions of UK's multinationalism shaped the country's COVID-19 response. In the third section, we demonstrate, using UK government press events, how the pandemic has highlighted the UK government's inconsistent—and at times neglectful—approach to the UK's multinationality. In the concluding section, we reiterate our conclusions about what the pandemic shows about the character of the UK as a multinational state.

The multinational condition

The defining characteristic of a multinational state is the *conditional* legitimacy of its political-territorial order.[3] In nation-states, the territory, the monistic character of the political community, and the key myths of that community, are taken for granted to such a degree that their social constructedness recedes from view. Public challenges to the territorial integrity of the state are more likely to elicit ridicule than apprehension.[4] By contrast, in multinational states, territorial integrity is not necessarily in constant jeopardy, but it is not taken for granted to the same degree. The legitimacy of the specific territorial-political order is conditional, particularly in those communities whose members consider their collective interests or their identity as being potentially sidelined within the common state framework. These may, but need not be, demographic minorities. If members of those communities can be persuaded that their interests are not being served, or their visions of the state not expressed in symbolically appropriate ways, they may call for the institutional reconfiguration of the state (for example, through greater autonomy or formal recognition). Should this not be forthcoming, they may withdraw their consent to being governed within the common state framework altogether, and pursue independence.

Scholarship on the multinational state has converged largely on the latter scenario— the potential for political crises that result either in peaceful secession of a territory, or in a violent clash motivated by self-determination contests. Since self-determination struggles become internationally prominent only when claimant communities make their demands for independence known—either through mass mobilization or by taking up arms—most of the scholarship on self-determination struggles tends to focus on the minority side of the equation.[5] Literature on the role of territorial autonomy and power-sharing almost universally emphasizes the influence of those institutional options on the political actions of minority/claimant communities.[6] A similar trend prevails in the more recent work on secession.[7]

Yet it is difficult to understand the multinational state without paying attention not only to the politics of minority nationalism, but also to the nationalism of majorities.[8] Minority claims, including secessionist ones, do not emerge in a vacuum. They are an iterative product of interaction between different political projects, both "within" communities and across them.[9] Indeed, the past decade or so has seen greater scholarly attention paid to majority nationalism in its various incarnations.[10] Especially important is the knowledge of how various communities and their representatives understand the institutions of the state.

Competing institutional visions are at the heart of the multinational predicament.[11] As noted at the start of this section, the multinational condition is partly a matter of institutional perceptions and institutional legitimacy. While members of minority nations diverge among themselves in terms of institutional preferences, they are, in the aggregate, far more likely to question the common state as a good in itself than are majorities. Their commitment to the state is, to put it differently, conditioned by the extent to which they believe that the state protects their interests and articulates and expresses their identity.[12] Majorities, on the other hand, are far more likely to identify with the entire state and to internalize it as "their own" more or less unconditionally.[13]

What we see as a result is a fairly predictable set of patterns. Minority nations tend to demand the right to self-government, either within the common state by way of territorial, and less often non-territorial, autonomy, or via external self-determination (secession). Central elites, normally drawn from the majority community, react in fairly predictable ways as well.[14] They nearly always resist secession, but are more likely to contemplate territorial autonomy. Indeed, almost all of the world's multinational states are characterized by some level of territorial decentralization or non-centralization. However, this autonomy is seldom accompanied by formal recognition of the state's multinationality, either in the constitutional sense or as a matter of public discourse. Of course, there is recognition of various lines of diversity, including regional and linguistic, among others, but this need not extend to institutionalization of the multinational principle. We see this even in some of the longest lasting multinational states such as Canada.[15]

The UK multinational state is even more exceptional when set against these trends. In effect, it has reversed the predictable pattern of accommodation: instead of starting with territorial autonomy and resisting recognition, it has been more willing to recognize, formally and rhetorically, its multinationalism, but has acknowledged this multinationality via territorial self-government only quite late. At the same time, since the establishment of devolved legislatures in 1998 and 1999, neither the UK political elite—notably members representing English constituencies—nor those who elect them, have been eager to acknowledge the separate political space in the UK's constituent nations, the near inevitability of intra-state policy variation flowing from jurisdictional competence over devolved policy areas, nor has there developed a strong institutional framework to coordinate across different governments. As we show in the rest of this article, the COVID-19 pandemic has exposed these features of the UK polity more clearly than before.

The impact of UK multinationalism on the pandemic response

The UK multinational state: a background

By contrast to most other state nationalisms, the UK variety has been quite comfortable in acknowledging the country's multinationality. British unionism has tended to be constitutively multinational. It has traditionally recognized national diversity and incorporated it into state symbols.[16] While one can point to the emergence of a British national identity,[17] this identity did not emerge to the exclusion of, say, Scottishness or Welshness,[18] though one might venture that in the English case, the fusion between the British and English identitarian dimensions was quite pronounced.[19] As we note in the foregoing section, this is typical of majority nationalism, but it is perhaps accentuated in the UK case by the particularly lopsided demographics of the country, as approximately 85% of its population resides in England. As importantly, unionism was neither the only nor necessarily the primary ideational marker for the population of Great Britain/UK. As Colley argues, both Protestantism and the empire were important cohesive forces that underpinned the UK multinational project.[20]

At the same time, however, unionists have for most of the past three centuries felt little need to supplement the UK's multinationalism with democratic institutional expression. The doctrine of parliamentary sovereignty militated against formal territorial autonomy and devolution for minority nations, most clearly seen during the 19th and early 20th century debates on Irish home rule.[21] The 19th century introduction of administrative devolution for Scotland and Wales ensured that civil servants developed policy for separate civil institutions—mostly obviously in Scotland given a separate education and legal system—but it was more than a hundred years before such policy reflected the political preferences of those living in the devolved territories rather than the wishes of the ministers elected by the UK electorate.[22] The delay was not merely due to the hostility on the part of the majority nation but also to hesitance on the part of the minority electorate.[23]

Devolution did not produce an *immediate* political backlash among the majority community, defined either as electors in England or British-identifiers in Scotland, Wales or Northern Ireland. This stands in contrast to the Canadian and Spanish reactions to symbolic reconstitution of those two states during the 1980s and 2000s, respectively.[24] At an elite level, none of the major state-wide parties made resentment against devolution a core aspect of their political strategy.[25] Indeed, all came to accept devolution as a positive development in their manifestos, though for different reasons and in different ways.[26]

The absence of sustained partisan opposition to devolution does not mean that the population of England has been indifferent to it. Over the past decade, scholars have started to outline the gathering resentment, or "devo-anxiety," among the English with respect to what they perceive as unfair advantages secured by the Scots in particular.[27] Both British and English identifiers believe that Scotland's share of public spending should be reduced and that Scottish MPs should not be allowed to vote on laws that affect England alone. At the same time, however, English opposition to devolution *as a matter of principle* is weak. While calls for an English Parliament are growing, particularly among those who prioritize an English national identity, the most popular institutional reform has been procedural rather than democratic, in the form of "English votes for English laws."[28] This provides an additional example of the hesitancy to offer or pursue democratic devolution for the national communities within the UK, with a preference for administrative solutions in the first instance.

To summarize, the UK governing elite has historically accepted the multinational character of the state as a cultural fact, while resisting institutional expression of that multinationality. Since the late 1990s, the process of devolution has led to increasing formal acceptance of institutionalized, multi-level multinationalism, but this institutionalization has been asymmetric, with important political and policy implications. While Scotland, Wales and Northern Ireland have developed their own institutions of governance, the demographically dominant population of England continues to be governed directly, without a coherent or comprehensive intermediate institutional layer. One could see this institutional asymmetry as an expression of the long-standing tendency to conflate England and the UK[29] that tends to view devolved policy choices as deviations from the norm.

The impact of the UK's institutional settlement on pandemic management and devolved politics

The manner in which devolution has been institutionalized has had important consequences for the management of the COVID-19 pandemic. The devolved governments have control over health, housing, education, and social care, but do not possess comprehensive fiscal or economic policy autonomy. Successive Scotland Acts (2012 and 2016) have broadened Scottish fiscal autonomy, but the scope for large-scale borrowing remains limited in size and purpose for both Scotland and Wales.[30] This means that while the devolved governments were in a position to pursue independent policy choices on many public health dimensions of the pandemic response in their territories, the UK government took the lead on the same in England and developed and implemented the fiscal response across the UK.

At the same time, the relationship between the devolved governments and the central administration has been poorly institutionalized, suggesting the relative lack of importance that the central government attaches to the multi-level character of the UK polity. By contrast to shared-rule federations like Germany or Switzerland, the devolved governments have no parliamentary representation at the center. Unlike other self-rule devolved or federal states, such as Canada and Spain, the formal intergovernmental channels of the UK are underdeveloped.[31] The Joint Ministerial Committee system, the UK's principal intergovernmental forum, is consultative and does not meet on a sufficiently regular basis to facilitate productive coordination in policy-making.[32] While the early response to the pandemic was coordinated, though not through the JMC, the central government subsequently charted its own course with far less collaboration with the devolved governments.[33]

The pandemic, combined with devolution in health care, but without strong institutionalization in the intergovernmental domain, shaped the devolved government response. While devolved governments implemented largely the same public health policies as the central government, and with similar health outcomes, they distinguished themselves from Westminster largely through differentiated timing in the implementation of those policies. Below, we focus on Scotland.

Throughout 2020 the SNP government in Scotland tended to implement more cautious measures sooner than the central government and typically loosened those measures later than the UK government. Table 1 summarizes some of these differences. The Scottish First Minister also provided daily press briefings, typically taking these herself rather than rotating the role with scientific advisors or other ministers. The Scottish electorate responded positively to both policy variation—which was more in line with cautious electorate preferences—and to the First Minister herself. By autumn 2020, 44% of Scots rated the Scottish government either 8, 9 or 10/10 (very well). Only nine percent gave the same rating to the UK government (with one in five rating them 0—very poorly—out of 10). As for the leaders, almost half (49%) rated Sturgeon's performance as 8, 9 or 10/10 while only 7% gave the same rating to Johnson. In part this is because nearly half of Scots rated Johnson's performance as 0, 1 or 2 out of 10. In short, half of Scots thought Sturgeon was performing in the top three categories of the scale, and half of Scots thought Johnson was in the bottom three categories of the scale.[34] It is important to note that in a more integrated intergovernmental system, the policy output might well have been more coordinated and the opportunity for variation restricted as a result.

At the same time, the pandemic has attracted attention to the legislative competence and policy choices of devolved actors like never before. Not only were different governments reacting simultaneously to the same external event, but their policy decisions had near immediate impact on citizen mobility. Thus, the lack of institutionalization of the

Table 1. A comparison of select UK, Scottish and Welsh governments' COVID-19 measures (March–December 2020).

Measure	UK government	Scottish government	Welsh government
Initial lockdown	23 March	23 March	23 March
Lockdown easing strategy published	11 May (late)	23 April (early)	24 April (early)
Lockdown easing (retail reopening)	15 June (early)	29 June (late)	22 June (late)
Lockdown easing (bars/ pubs/ restaurants reopened)	4 July (early)	15 July (late)	13 July (late)
Lockdown easing (gyms reopened)	25 July (early)	31 August (late)	3 August (late)
Mandatory mask wearing introduced	24 July (late)	10 July (early)	14 September (very late)
Lockdown easing (lifting restrictions on foreign arrivals)	10 July (25 July reimposition of quarantine on arrivals from Spain)	10 July (but more restrictive, Spain/Serbia left out)	10 July (same as England)
Renewed restrictions on households	14 September ("rule of 6")	14 September ("rule of 6", but limited to 2 households)	7 September (different regime, local lockdowns instead of household restrictions across the board)
Renewed restrictions on business	14 October (late—pubs/ bars but not restos closed in Tier 3, only applicable to Liverpool City Reg.)	9 October (early—pubs/ bars/restos closed in Central Belt (majority of population covered))	N/A (early lockdown reintroduced earlier than elsewhere—see below)
Full lockdown reintroduced	5 November (early, but only until 2 December, reintroduced)	26 December/5 January (late)	23 October (early, for 17 days only, reintroduced 20 December, with Christmas exemption)

multi-level system of governance combined with the pandemic to offer a unique opportunity to all devolved governments to boost their profile among their respective electorates. In the Scottish case in particular, this appeared to accelerate public support for independence, increasing since the 2019 election but routinely topping 50% since March of 2020.[35] Likewise, the pandemic appears to have influenced a wider range of policy decisions. The SNP campaigned in the 2021 election on a commitment to holding a second independence referendum "once the COVID crisis had passed."[36] Since both the health and economic effects of the pandemic are likely to linger for some time to come, this commitment gives the returning SNP government ample flexibility over the referendum issue.

The situation in Wales parallels the Scottish developments in some important ways. As in Scotland, the pandemic offered an opportunity to evaluate simultaneous policy variation given devolved competence over health. As Table 1 shows, just as in Scotland, the Welsh government took a more cautious approach to the pandemic management. While opinion polls showed greater support in Wales than Scotland for the UK government's handling of the pandemic, polling on leaders showed far stronger support for the performance of Welsh First Minister Mark Drakeford, and falling support for Prime Minister Boris Johnson.[37] Drakeford, and the party he leads, Welsh Labour, have pursued a markedly different approach to the UK government than Sturgeon and the SNP.[38]

While support for independence in Wales has increased, now regularly reaching between a quarter and a third of those sampled, this has not translated into increased support for Plaid Cymru.[39] Welsh Labour has emerged from the pandemic as the party best seen to stand up for Wales. Thus, in Wales, the combination of pandemic and the specific political configuration may have strengthened the image of the devolved government, but it has also resulted in a pro-union government calling for substantial constitutional reform of the union.

The impact of the pandemic on the UK's multinationalism

Above we demonstrated how devolved governments' pandemic management intersected with the politics of national identity in Scotland and Wales. In this section, we show that the pandemic has exposed more clearly than before the degree to which the Anglo-British political and media elites elide England and the UK. Put differently, the pandemic has thrown into sharper relief the relatively low salience of the multi-level character of the UK multinational polity. We start with the discussion of popular understanding of the multi-level system and the barriers to better understanding of it. We then turn to the way in which the UK elites have framed the central government's response to the pandemic by examining Downing Street press conferences in March and April of 2020.

The asymmetric nature of devolution has always proved a challenge to UK voters for three reasons. First, different devolved legislatures had different levels of policy control so any heuristic shortcuts individuals might employ in federal states would be of limited use in an asymmetric situation. Put another way, knowing what was happening in one's own territory would prove a relatively poor guide to what was happening in other parts of the state. To some degree, this reflects the different origins of the legislatures, with devolution to Northern Ireland arriving thanks to an international treaty, and the different devolution settlements in Scotland and Wales the result of referendums following a Labour victory in 1997 and reflecting different levels of enthusiasm within the populations for constitutional change. Second, the legislative competence of the devolved institutions has changed since 1999, most dramatically in Wales where the legislature acquired primary legislative powers following the Government of Wales Act in 2006, but also in Scotland after successive Scotland Acts expanded the legislature's capacity particularly around tax.[40] Even if a voter had explored in depth the legislative competences of the Scottish Parliament in the year leading up to the 2014 referendum, they would have found significant changes as the full powers of the Scotland Acts 2012 and 2016 came into force in the years after the referendum. Those not living in Scotland or Wales could be forgiven for not following these debates attentively.

Third, particularly for those in England, media reporting about the legislative competence of devolved regions, and UK government communications about the territorial reach of its legislation, has not aided public understanding. Government announcements frequently occlude, whether by omission or design, the England-only aspects of policy changes, announcing new plans for hospitals or schools without clarifying that this applies to England alone. Such is the level of frustration that it has prompted two high profile Twitter campaigns, the Welsh-based @thatsdevolved, which attempts to correct misleading government communications and news reports, and #sayEngland, which seeks to highlight when the territorial reach of England-only policy is unclear or hidden. The post-devolution elision of England/Britain/UK by parties and government is a long-standing and well documented phenomenon in UK politics.[41]

Related to this is the demographic dominance of England. Often cited as a potential obstacle to governance arrangements, it is relevant here for the center of gravity for news reporting. England-based newspapers and network news (from BBC, ITV or Sky) have considerable reach within Scotland, Wales and Northern Ireland, but the dominance of the English audience means coverage is often unreflectively Anglo-British, without much interrogation into whether the news item applies to the whole of the UK, Britain, or England. This list obviously includes a combination of effects. Some would be present in any asymmetric system (the absence of heuristic cues, for example). Still, the bulk of these are a result of the British manifestation of asymmetric devolution, namely serial *ad hocery*[42] and unclear communications, in part exacerbated by England's demographic dominance.

If one does not live in Scotland and does not know what the Scottish Parliament controls, and then reads English newspapers that report little on any of the devolved legislatures or the territorial limits of Westminster's domestic policy, then opportunities for learning are limited. Little wonder that the electorates across Britain make different judgements (and errors) about legislative competence. Scots tend to under-estimate Holyrood's powers, and English voters tend to over-estimate it. The result is that 20 years after devolution, the knowledge of legislative competence and the extent of policy variation is patchy, particularly in England, and there is continued support for policy uniformity across the whole of the state. The first of these is a direct result of the asymmetrical nature of the settlement given the absence of reliable cues. On the issue of knowledge of policy variation, however, the notion that citizens in symmetrical federal states have a detailed understanding of policy variation across the constituent states is perhaps optimistic.

What we find in the United Kingdom, however, is that the presence of high-profile policy deviation in the devolved legislatures is accompanied by high support for those policies in the devolved regions. This includes free university tuition in Scotland, free prescriptions in all three devolved territories, a free bus pass for over 55s in Scotland, as well as free personal care for the elderly.[43] It is perhaps not surprising, then, that support for policy uniformity is high, but that it has both principled and practical considerations—support for policy uniformity in principle out of a sense of social solidarity, and practical support because people want the same entitlements as the most generous options on offer.

This support is highest in England, with 70–80% of English respondents favoring uniform policy provision across the United Kingdom depending on whether this includes tuition fees, prescription charges, care for the elderly, and the sentencing for young offenders. It is not, however, a purely English phenomenon, with substantial proportions of those in territories with devolved legislatures also preferring policy uniformity across the state. As a result, the UK is home to a devolution paradox: large proportions of the citizenry view devolved legislatures as legitimate, and indeed in many cases wish for more power to be devolved, but substantial proportions of those same people want policy to be the same.[44] Put another way, people in the UK want devolved legislatures to have the freedom to make identical decisions.[45] This background is important to help explain the various patterns we see in the UK government response to the COVID pandemic. In what follows we explore attention to the multi-level nature of the UK in communication of COVID developments, including communications from Westminster and resulting media coverage.

The COVID-19 crisis demonstrates the limits to the governing elite's perception of the UK as a multinational and multi-level state. This is in evidence when we examine the manner in which the UK government communicated with the UK general public about the pandemic. In response to the developing public health crisis, the Prime Minister, often accompanied by his scientific advisors or other government ministers, began delivering regular press conferences on 3 March 2020. These consisted of prepared statements, followed by questions from journalists, and were broadcast live. The following discussion draws on an analysis of each of these events throughout the first two months of the pandemic in March and April 2020. We use this time period deliberately, as the early weeks of grappling with a global pandemic show the UK government's reaction at its most instinctual, before outside actors shaped its response. They offer, therefore, a truer, unguarded representation of the UK government's approach to the multi-national, multi-level character of the UK. Daily press conferences about a single event are unprecedented in peace time, which inhibits comparison over time, but they offer an ideal opportunity to evaluate how, in the midst of a global pandemic, the UK government reflected or sought to accommodate the multinational character of the UK.

The UK Government's COVID press conferences provided important early guidance about, for example, hand washing, additional advice for those over 70s, and later maintaining a safe distance, as well as updates on infection rates. An analysis of each of the prepared statement portions of the first two months of press conferences (3 March to 30 April inclusive) provides an opportunity to assess (a) references to the four territories explicitly (or the three First Ministers in Scotland, Wales and Northern Ireland) and (b) clarity on the territorial reach of data, new policy, announcements or advice. The results reveal that members of the electorate attempting to track which rules and advice applied where and when would have found that task a difficult one.

In March, the Prime Minister made reference to Scotland, Wales or Northern Ireland only twice, by referring to the other first ministers, and both times that he was planning to, or had recently met with them. By April there were three explicit mentions of the devolved territories. On 8 April, Rishi Sunak announced £60 million of funding through the Barnett formula to help Scotland, Wales and Northern Ireland.[46] On 21 April, Health and Social Care Secretary Matt Hancock thanked a range of public bodies and government departments, with a reference to "the devolved administrations and territorial offices" appearing midway through the list. Later in the month the Transport Secretary mentioned Northern Ireland in relation to support for ferry and air links to Belfast and Derry. There were no further mentions of Scotland or Wales and no mentions of the first ministers of the three devolved administrations during this period.

When we examine the territorial reach of items covered in the briefings we can look for two things: first, whether it is possible to infer what the territorial reach is (by reference to a legislative competence that is reserved, for example) and second, whether the territorial reach is explicitly identified. For example, in the first press conference Boris Johnson announced the existence of coronavirus action plan (if not its content) and stated that it applied to the whole of the UK. The 12 March statement about not closing schools, by contrast, would have been a decision for England only (since education is devolved in Scotland, Wales and Northern Ireland) but this was not clarified.

In general, UK government spokespersons almost never clarified when an announcement or a measure applied only to England. Thus, the previously mentioned announcement about schools on 12 March, or the decision 6 days later to close them, did not state the measures applied only to England. The call for retired healthcare professionals to return to their posts (and the announcement 5 days later that 7,500 former clinicians were returning to service) likewise applied only to the NHS in England (as health is devolved), but this was not specified either. Indeed, throughout March, only one of the items that applied only to England was explicitly identified as such: Alok Sharma's announcement on 28th March that English councils (local governments) were providing direct funding to businesses affected by lockdown. This was not a sign that the UK government had begun clarifying the territorial reach of various measures. One day later, Robert Jenrick's announcement of strategic coordination centers (which applied throughout England) was described as providing support throughout "this country," without specifying what the "country" in question was. On 31 March Michael Gove employed the same vague term when announcing over 8,000 ventilators were being deployed. By contrast, the UK government clarified more frequently when items applied to the whole of the UK, doing so 33 times in March. The most frequent instances of this were for data on testing, hospitalization and deaths, or for the number of repatriated citizens.

In April, England-only items were flagged more often but only marginally so. This included Alok Sharma's 1st April announcement that English councils had received more than £12 billion for financial assistance to small businesses, and Matt Hancock's announcement the next day that 5.7% of doctors in England were off work due to COVID. The following day, he noted there were over 2,000 critical care beds available in "this country," which we can assume applies to England. By 5th April he indeed clarified that the critical care bed figures were for NHS England, but a week later was referring to 121,000 gowns that had been delivered around "the country." This lack of clarity plagued announcements about the R value as well (16 April).

Across the entire month, England-only items were clarified as such nine times. At times this was partly because the organization involved had the word "England" in its name (Public Health England, Highways England). If we look at items that applied to the whole of the UK, again the territorial reach of this was cited more than for the England-only items, but less often than the month before. As in March, references to the UK typically surfaced in figures for testing, positive cases and hospitalization. In short, during both months there was a consistent lack of clarity on the territorial reach of a range of announcements, including laptops for students so they could study at home (presumably referring to England), the number of extra hospital beds (presumably England), the existence or extension of the coronavirus jobs retention scheme (all UK), or the number of items of PPE distributed, but that in general government spokespeople

Table 2. Attention to territorial reach and devolution in Number 10 press conferences, March–April 2020.

	Explicit references to the four territories in the UK or three First Ministers in Scotland, W, NI	Explicit reference to the territorial reach of policy
March (22 press events, 121 items)	2	England-only 1 GB/UK 33
April (30 press events)	4	England-only 9 GB/UK 27

showed greater efforts at clarifying when things applied to the whole of the UK than when they applied to England alone.

Two examples help to emphasize just how easily central government representatives shift between the UK and England-only frame of reference, further contributing to confusion about the constitutional framework of the multi-level state. On 22 April Dominic Raab thanked the Ministry of Defence and Defence Secretary Ben Wallace for their efforts. Those watching might or might not have been aware that defence is a reserved competence, and the MoD has installations across the UK. Raab then went on to provide examples of MoD assistance, which included delivering the new Nightingale hospitals[47] and the new local resilience forums to deliver PPE. The Nightingale hospitals, however, have been established in England only, while the local resilience forums are also England only, with similar but differently-named entities in Scotland and Wales. This was therefore a UK-wide defence ministry delivering England-only contributions. This is obviously entirely normal, but the announcement lacked clarification that the various achievements were for England rather than the UK.

Raab also noted that "People used to joke in *this country* [italics added] that you could never build a hospital that quickly. Well, we didn't just build one, we built seven and we thank our armed forces for helping to make that happen." There were of course ten temporary hospitals built in the UK, of which seven were in England. The example helps to illustrate the sleight of hand by which the territorial frame of references shifts from the UK to England with very little clarity. The following day, Matt Hancock announced the need to make progress on test, track and trace, with a goal of 100,000 tests per day. No territorial frame of reference was provided but he later explained the desire to "make it faster and simpler for any essential worker in England who needs a test to get a test." This was accompanied by information on how to book a test, followed by "it's all part of getting Britain back on her feet." England and Britain are either so clearly merged in the minds of central government ministers that distinguishing between them makes little sense, or they are willfully constructed as such for public consumption (Table 2).

Faced with significant obfuscation, both in terms of what the devolved governments were doing, or when announcements applied only to England, it is perhaps not surprising that media coverage of the multi-level aspects of the UK coronavirus response were similarly hazy. Research from Cardiff University's journalism school demonstrates that a lack of clarity over different policy choices across the UK led to considerable public confusion.[48] This was a direct result of imprecise government messaging, inconsistent media attention to the relationship between reserved and devolved powers, as well as four-nation differences in evening news reports. The confusion was sown not by difference, but by the lack of communication about that difference.

This lack of attention did not go unnoticed. Ofcom, the UK's regulatory agency for communication, issued three notes to broadcasters on Coronavirus reporting in March, April, and May, warning of the dangers of misleading information. Much of this focused on the perils of distorted information with respect to medical advice. There was no follow up on this particular issue in April, but by May 2020 Ofcom warned that care should be taken with

> statements about public health advice on Coronavirus which may not apply to all four nations in the UK, given the variations in official guidance between the nations. Care should be taken to ensure that viewers and listeners are made aware in an appropriate manner of the different approaches taken by public authorities in England, Wales, Scotland and/or Northern Ireland in areas such as social distancing requirements.[49]

This suggests a slow awakening in some quarters, not about the asymmetric nature of devolution but the very existence of devolution and the capacity for variation within the state. This is one of a number of ways in which the coronavirus crisis has attracted attention to the extent of and consequences of devolved legislative competence, a process that, arguably, should have occurred shortly after 1999.

Conclusion

Evaluating the effects of an event on a political system while that event is ongoing is at once tempting and perilous. On the one hand, it is difficult to believe that an event as seismic as the COVID-19 pandemic would not have *some* sort of political consequence on a political system, in this case, awareness of, or preferences for, the multinational settlement in the United Kingdom, or make clear long simmering tensions. On the other hand, whatever political tendencies we may observe at such an exceptional time may be subject to change once society returns to some degree of normalcy. If we are to take Capoccia and Kelemen seriously, however, even the realistic *possibility* of a major political shift, whether or not that shift materializes, nevertheless may constitute a critical juncture.[50]

In this article, we opt for a relatively safe strategy. We document what had been happening over the course of the first stage of COVID-19 pandemic response, including how the UK multinational and asymmetric settlement has influenced the government response (part I), and what the response tells us about the character of that settlement (part II). In some ways, the pandemic has further revealed a level of indifference among the Anglo-British elites about the multi-level character of the state. Below we speculate, cautiously, about the potential future consequences of these patterns on the multinational system of the United Kingdom.

The interaction of the COVID-19 crisis with the peculiar (by international comparison) asymmetric territorial arrangement of the UK state has made it possible for devolved governments to differentiate—at times dissociate—themselves from the central government's response. The fact that health care is a devolved responsibility has provided a platform for devolved political actors to distinguish themselves on policy choices, on timing, and on communications. While much of the variation on policy and timing has been, as we have shown, very much at the margins, at times limited by the particular distribution of legislative competence, the daily appearance of sub-state devolved politicians has served to sustain perceptions of competence in devolved administrations. This is not a blunt rallying around the flag effect, for the same levels of trust and competence have not been extended to the UK government or Prime Minister. Obviously, devolved administrations are presiding over infection rates and death tolls that, in an international context highlight just how badly hit the entire UK has been by coronavirus. The devolved administrations have benefited, though, from a comparison with English rates and a UK government that has presided over figures that have been, at times, the worst in Europe. There are obviously many reasons why individuals choose to support independence but it is worth noting that support for independence in Wales rose dramatically after March 2020 and accelerated over the same period in Scotland, routinely crossing a significant psychological barrier of 50%.

At the same time, the pandemic has revealed more clearly the manner in which the London-based media and political elites view the UK state and its institutions. We show that, at least during the first two months of the pandemic, the UK government frequently failed to specify the territorial reach of policy measures it was announcing. The UK Government's press briefings also seldom mentioned the devolved jurisdictions. It was frequently unclear whether a specific announcement applied to the entirety of the UK or some part of it, though a closer look reveals frequent conflation of measures applied to England and the UK both by design and by default. This has led to some confusion among the public with respect to which set of rules one ought to follow. It is beyond the scope of this particular paper to explore in depth the potential consequences of that confusion. More importantly from the perspective of our analysis, it reinforces the point that the UK governing elites tend to view England and the UK interchangeably, and (or perhaps because) they do not appear to take seriously the multi-level character of the UK multinational state. In this sense, the pandemic has proved not so much a catalyst as a mirror for the multi-level character of the UK multinational state.

Notes

1. Ailsa Henderson and Richard Wyn Jones, *Englishness: The Political Force Transforming Britain* (Oxford: Oxford University Press, 2021).
2. We cover Wales in less detail although we explore very important implications of the pandemic there. Northern Ireland is left out entirely since key issues associated with its place in the UK stem and the fallout of Brexit would require an article of its own.
3. Karlo Basta, *The Symbolic State: Minority Recognition, Majority Backlash, and Secession in Multinational Countries* (Kingston: McGill-Queen's University Press, 2021).
4. Ian Lustick, "Thresholds of Opportunity and Barriers to Change in the Right-Sizing of States," in *Rightsizing the State: The Politics of Moving Borders*, edited by Brendan O'Leary, Ian Lustick, and Thomas M. Callaghy (Oxford; New York: Oxford University Press, 2001), 85.
5. Thus, the debate on integration versus accommodation tends to emphasize the way particular institutions—whether federal or power sharing—shape the political actions of claimant (normally minority) communities (John McGarry, Brendan O'Leary, and Richard Simeon, "Integration or Accommodation? The Enduring Debate in Conflict Regulation," in *Constitutional Design for Divided Societies: Integration or Accommodation?*, edited by Sujit Choudhry (Oxford: Oxford University Press, 2008)).
6. The literature is too vast to cite here. For a sample of integrationist arguments—scholars who believe that institutional accommodation increases the likelihood that claimant groups

will try a radical break with the status quo, including secession and rebellion, see Valerie Bunce, *Subversive Institutions: The Design and the Destruction of Socialism and the State* (Cambridge, UK: Cambridge University Press, 1999); Erin K. Jenne, "The Paradox of Ethnic Partition: Lessons from de Facto Partition in Bosnia and Kosovo," *Regional & Federal Studies* 19, no. 2 (2009): 273–89; Philip G. Roeder, *Where Nation-States Come from: Institutional Change in the Age of Nationalism* (Princeton, NJ: Princeton University Press, 2007). For accommodationist arguments—the notion that institutionalizing and accommodating national difference is more likely to dampen minority nationalism, see Nancy Bermeo, "The Import of Institutions," *Journal of Democracy* 13, no. 2 (2002): 96–110; John McGarry and Brendan O'Leary, "Federation as a Method of Ethnic Conflict Regulation," in *From Power Sharing to Democracy: Post-Conflict Institutions in Ethnically Divided Societies*, edited by Sid Noel (Kingston: McGill-Queen's University Press, 2005), 263–96; Lars-Erik Cederman, Simon Hug, Andreas Schädel, and Julian Wucherpfennig, "Territorial Autonomy in the Shadow of Conflict: Too Little, Too Late?," *American Political Science Review* 109, no. 2 (2015): 354–70. "Situationalist" scholars, those who point to specific conditions under which institutions may or may not alleviate minority claims, similarly tend to focus on minority/claimant communities. See, for instance, Kristin M. Bakke, *Decentralization and Intrastate Struggles: Chechnya, Punjab, and Québec* (New York: Cambridge University Press, 2015); Dawn Brancati, *Peace by Design: Managing Intrastate Conflict Through Decentralization* (Oxford: Oxford University Press, 2009).

7. Scholars exploring structural factors (Elise Giuliano, "Secessionism from the Bottom up: Democratization, Nationalism, and Local Accountability in the Russian Transition," *World Politics* 58, no. 2 (2006): 276–310; David S. Siroky and John Cuffe, "Lost Autonomy, Nationalism and Separatism," *Comparative Political Studies* 48, no. 1 (2015): 3–34; Jason Sorens, *Secessionism: Identity, Interest, and Strategy* (Montreal; Ithaca: McGill-Queen's University Press, 2012)), as well as those looking at individual characteristics (Maria Jose Hierro and Didac Queralt, "The Divide over Independence: Explaining Preferences for Secession in an Advanced Open Economy," *American Journal of Political Science* 65, no. 2 (2021): 422–42; Matthew Mendelsohn, "Rational Choice and Socio-Psychological Explanation for Opinion on Quebec Sovereignty," *Canadian Journal of Political Science* 36, no. 3 (2003): 511–37; Diego Muro and Martijn C. Vlaskamp, "How Do Prospects of EU Membership Influence Support for Secession? A Survey Experiment in Catalonia and Scotland," *West European Politics* 39, no. 6 (2016): 1115–38) frequently focus on the political activities and demands of minority nations.

8. André Lecours and Geneviève Nootens, eds., *Dominant Nationalism, Dominant Ethnicity: Identity, Federalism, and Democracy* (Bruxelles: P.I.E. Peter Lang, 2009); Alain Gagnon, Geneviève Nootens, and André Lecours, eds., *Contemporary Majority Nationalism. Studies in Nationalism and Ethnic Conflict* (Montreal; Ithaca: McGill-Queen's University Press, 2011).

9. Karlo Basta, "The State between the Minority and Majority Nationalism: Decentralization, Symbolic Recognition, and Secessionist Crises in Spain and Canada," *Publius: The Journal of Federalism* 48, no. 1 (2018): 51–75; Basta, *The Symbolic State*; Philip Resnick, "Hubris and Melancholy in Multinational States," *Nations and Nationalism* 14, no. 4 (2008): 789–807.

10. Daniel Cetrà and Coree Brown Swan, "State and Majority Nationalism in Plurinational States: Responding to Challenges from Below," *Nationalism and Ethnic Politics* 26, no. 1 (2020): 1–7; Eric Kaufmann and Oded Haklai, "Dominant Ethnicity: From Minority to Majority," *Nations and Nationalism* 14, no. 4 (2008): 743–67; Gagnon et al., *Contemporary Majority Nationalism*; Lecours and Nootens, *Dominant Nationalism, Dominant Ethnicity*.

11. For an underappreciated treatment of the variability of such visions within minority national communities, see Jaime Lluch, *Visions of Sovereignty: Nationalism and Accommodation in Multinational Democracies* (Philadelphia: University of Pennsylvania Press, 2014).

12. Nicola McEwen and André Lecours, "Voice or Recognition? Comparing Strategies for Accommodating Territorial Minorities in Multinational States," *Commonwealth & Comparative Politics* 46, no. 2 (2008): 220–43; Wilfried Swenden, "Territorial Strategies for Managing Plurinational States," in *Routledge Handbook of Regionalism and Federalism*, edited by John Loughlin, John Kincaid, and Wilfried Swenden (New York: Routledge, 2013).

13. Basta, *The Symbolic State*; Zachary Elkins and John Sides, "Can Institutions Build Unity in Multiethnic States?," *American Political Science Review* 101, no. 4 (2007): 693–708; Henderson and Wyn Jones, *Englishness*; Christian Staerklé, Jim Sidanius, Eva G. T. Green, and Ludwin E. Molina, "Ethnic Minority-Majority Asymmetry in National Attitudes around the World: A Multilevel Analysis," *Political Psychology* 31, no. 4 (2010): 491–519.

14. John McGarry, "Asymmetry in Federations, Federacies and Unitary States," *Ethnopolitics* 6, no. 1 (2007): 105–16; Philip Resnick, "Hubris and Melancholy in Multinational States," *Nations and Nationalism* 14, no. 4 (2008): 789–807.

15. Karlo Basta, "Performing Canadian State Nationalism through Federal Symmetry," *Nationalism and Ethnic Politics* 26, no. 1 (2020): 66–84.

16. Michael Keating, "Reforging the Nation: Britain, Scotland and the Crisis of Unionism," in *Multinational Federalism: Problems and Prospects*, edited by Michel Seymour and Alain Gagnon (Houndmills, Basingstoke, Hampshire; New York: Palgrave Macmillan, 2012), 109.

17. Linda Colley, "Britishness and Otherness: An Argument," *The Journal of British Studies* 31, no. 4 (1992): 309–29.

18. Graeme Morton, *Unionist Nationalism: Governing Urban Scotland 1830-60* (East Linton: Tuckwell Press, 1999).

19. Henderson and Wyn Jones, *Englishness*.

20. Colley, "Britishness and Otherness: An Argument."

21. Vernon Bogdanor, *Devolution in the United Kingdom* (Oxford: Oxford University Press, 2001), 29.

22. The Irish question is qualitatively different from either the Scottish or the Welsh one, in part due to the salience of the religious divide well into the 19th century and, in some instances, beyond it (David Hempton, *Religion and Political Culture in Britain and Ireland: From the Glorious Revolution to the Decline of Empire* (Cambridge: Cambridge University Press, 1996); John Wolffe, *God and Greater Britain: Religion and National Life in Britain and Ireland, 1843-1945* (London; New York: Routledge, 1994)).

23. Although government decisions about process, not least the quota for devolution referendums in 1979, did not provide clear opportunities for the expression of demands for change.

24. Basta, "The State between the Minority and Majority Nationalism."

25. Arthur Aughey, "Anxiety and Injustice: The Anatomy of Contemporary English Nationalism," *Nations and Nationalism* 16, no. 3 (2010): 506–24; Susan Condor, "Devolution and National Identity: The Rules of English (Dis)Engagement," *Nations and Nationalism* 16, no. 3 (2010): 525–43.

26. Coree Brown Swan and Daniel Cetrà, "Why Stay Together? State Nationalism and Justifications for State Unity in Spain and the UK," *Nationalism and Ethnic Politics* 26, no. 1 (2020): 46–65, 50.

27. Richard Wyn Jones, Guy Lodge, Ailsa Henderson, and Daniel Wincott, *The Dog that Finally Barked: England as an Emerging Political Community* [report] (London: Institute for Public Policy Research, 2012); Richard Wyn Jones, Guy Lodge, Charlie Jeffery, Glenn Gottfried, Roger Scully, Ailsa Henderson, and Daniel Wincott, *England and Its Two Unions: The Anatomy of a Nation and Its Discontents* [report] (London: Institute for Public Policy Research, 2013); Ailsa Henderson, Charlie Jeffery, Robert Liñeira, Roger Scully, Daniel Wincott, and Richard Wyn Jones, "England, Englishness and Brexit," *The Political Quarterly* 87, no. 2 (2016): 187–99; Henderson and Wyn Jones, *Englishness*.

28. Henderson et al., "England, Englishness and Brexit."

29. Henderson and Wyn Jones, *Englishness*.

30. Patrizio Lecca, Peter G. McGregor, and Kim Swales, "Taxes and Spending," in *A Wealthier, Fairer Scotland: The Political Economy of Constitutional Change*, edited by Michael Keating (Edinburgh: Edinburgh University Press Ltd, 2017), 29.

31. Nicola McEwen and Bettina Petersohn, "Between Autonomy and Interdependence: The Challenges of Shared Rule after the Scottish Referendum," *The Political Quarterly* 86, no. 2 (2015): 192–200.

32. Nicola McEwen, Michael Kenny, Jack Sheldon, and Coree Brown Swan, "Intergovernmental Relations in the UK: Time for a Radical Overhaul?," *The Political Quarterly* 91, no. 3 (2020): 632–40, 1.

33. House of Commons Scottish Affairs Committee. "Coronavirus and Scotland: Interim Report on Intergovernmental Working," 2020, 14, https://www.centreonconstitutionalchange.ac.uk/publications/coronavirus-and-scotland-interim-report-intergovernmental-working.

34. Progress Scotland poll by Panelbase, fieldwork 25 September–5 October 2020.

35. Mure Dickie, "Sturgeon Vows to Hold 'Legal' Second Independence Vote in Scotland." *Financial Times*, 24 January 2021, Web edition, https://www.ft.com/content/93402eaf-9f48-43f7-bf59-981b8273d2e6.

36. SNP's 11-point plan in essence entails passing a referendum legislation and then daring the UK government to challenge it in court or to allow it via Section 30 order as it did for the 2014 referendum (Michael Russell, "This Is the SNP's Routemap to a Scottish Independence Referendum in Full," *The National*, 23 January 2021, 12, Web edition, https://www.thenational.scot/news/19033561.snps-road-scottish-independence-referendum-plan-full/.).

37. Roger Awan-Scully, "Welsh Tories Are Misreading the Mood on Covid." *The Spectator*, 5 June 2020, 2020. https://www.spectator.co.uk/article/welsh-tories-are-misreading-the-public-mood-on-covid.

38. *BBC News*. 2021. "Mark Drakeford Says UK Must Be Radically Redrawn to Survive," 14 January, 2021, sec. Wales politics. https://www.bbc.com/news/uk-wales-politics-55649017.

39. Steven Morris, "Westminster Warned as Poll Shows Record Backing for Welsh Independence." *The Guardian*, 4 March 2021, Web edition, https://www.theguardian.com/uk-news/2021/mar/04/westminster-warned-as-poll-shows-record-backing-for-welsh-independence.

40. Lecca et al., "Taxes and Spending," in *A Wealthier, Fairer Scotland*.

41. Henderson and Wyn Jones, *Englishness*, Michael Kenny, *The Politics of English Nationhood* (Oxford: Oxford University Press, 2014).

42. Henderson and Wyn Jones, *Englishness*.

43. Michael Keating, Linda Stevenson, Paul Cairney, and Katherine Taylor, "Does Devolution Make a Difference? Legislative Output and Policy Divergence in Scotland," *The Journal of Legislative Studies* 9, no. 3 (2003): 110–39.

44. Ailsa Henderson, Charlie Jeffery, Daniel Wincott, and Richard Wyn Jones, "Reflections on the 'Devolution Paradox': A Comparative Examination of Multi-Level Citizenship," *Regional Studies* 47, no. 3 (2013): 303–22; Henderson and Wyn Jones, *Englishness*.

45. Ailsa Henderson, "The Freedom to Make Identical Decisions: The Devolution Paradox" in *Sex, Lies and the Ballot Box II*, edited by Philip Cowley and Robert Ford (London: Biteback Press, 2016), 181–4.

46. The Formula is a mechanism for the allocation of UK Treasury's funds to devolved jurisdictions (Linda Ferguson, Peter McGregor, Kim Swales, and Karen Turner, *The Regional Distribution of Public Expenditures in the UK: An Exposition and Critique of the Barnett Formula*. Discussion Paper (Glasgow: University of Strathclyde, 2003)).

47. These are temporary critical care facilities established to boost the critical care capacity in England.

48. Stephen Cushion, Nikki Soo, Maria Kyriakidou, and Marina Morani, "Different Lockdown Rules in the Four Nations Are Confusing the Public," *LSE Blog*, 2020, https://blogs.lse.ac.uk/covid19/2020/05/22/different-lockdown-rules-in-the-four-nations-are-confusing-the-public/.

49. Ofcom, "Ofcom Broadcast and On Demand Bulletin (2020) Note to Broadcasters Coronavirus Update," 2020, https://www.ofcom.org.uk/__data/assets/pdf_file/0033/195873/Note-to-broadcasters-Coronavirus-update.pdf.
50. Giovanni Capoccia and R. Daniel Kelemen, "The Study of Critical Junctures: Theory, Narrative, and Counterfactuals in Historical Institutionalism," *World Politics* 59, no. 3 (2007): 341–69.

ORCID

Karlo Basta   http://orcid.org/0000-0002-1526-0644
Ailsa Henderson   http://orcid.org/0000-0003-1818-5675

Nationalism and COVID in Belgium: A Surprisingly United Response in a Divided Federal Country

Dave Sinardet and Jade Pieters

ABSTRACT

Belgium is considered as a very divided multinational and federal state, with conflicts between representatives of its two main language communities regularly threatening its sheer existence. Moreover, at the outbreak of the COVID 19-crisis, Belgium was in the middle of a political crisis: ten months of failed attempts to form a new federal government left a minority caretaker government to deal with the crisis. When the second wave arrived, a new federal government was formed but its composition was strongly different than the Flemish government, which was lead by the Flemish-nationalist N-VA, a situation of incongruence between governments that generally reinforces political conflicts within Belgium. All this means that a very fragmented, divisive and conflictual COVID-response could be expected. Therefore, it is surprising that the response was largely uniform and national response. There was a political consensus that measures should be the same over the entire territory. This article details the institutions, policies and communication that created this national response and also explains the reasons for it. It also focuses on the problems that the distribution of competences posed to execute the response and what it means for the nationalist movement as well as for possible future constitutional reform.

Introduction

The coronavirus poses an important paradox: while it led to a global pandemic, constituting the same major health threat for the world population across all possible borders, policy responses, as well as media coverage on them, were largely contained within the realms of the nation-state. The first wave of the pandemic even saw the closing of national borders within the European Union, which thus became "hard" again, regaining a significance no one could have imagined possible.

Also, within many multi-national and/or federal states, COVID-19 often exacerbated preexisting territorial and cultural divisions. Countries like Spain, the UK, the US, or even Germany and Switzerland have seen important differences and often conflicts arise between their constituent units on the precise policy responses to give to the health care crisis. This contribution will look at the effect of COVID-19 on what is often considered to be one of the most divided and conflictious multinational countries: Belgium. The analysis covers the period from the start of the pandemic to May 2021.

Given Belgium's very divided federal structure and political system, one could expect the country to be even more badly equipped than some of its other multinational and/ or federal counterparts to develop an efficient policy response to COVID-19. Especially since the division of competences on health care between the federal state and the regions and communities is probably one of Belgium's most complex and problematic. To make things worse, the global pandemic also caught Belgium in the middle of a political crisis: ten months after the most recent federal election, Belgium was still very far from forming a new federal government, leaving a minority caretaker government with a novice prime minister to deal with arguably the largest crisis since the second world war. Moreover, this caretaker government was not composed of the same parties as the regional governments, a situation of incongruence between governments which in Belgium traditionally leads to conflicts and which remained when Belgium got a new federal government around the start of the second wave. And last but not least, the Flemish government was led by a (radical) Flemish-nationalist party which became the main federal opposition party and has an ideological vocation to show that the Belgian state does not function. Moreover, this situation was the result of elections where the combined score of (radical) Flemish-nationalist parties had strongly increased.

Before looking at the actual policy response of Belgium to the COVID-19 crisis we will first explain in more detail the institutional, societal, and political context in which this occurred, which is necessary to understand the intricacies of the response itself.

A "multinational" divided country in the middle of a political crisis

In academic literature, as well as in public and political discourse, Belgium is often characterized as a (severely) divided country,[1] the sheer existence of which is threatened by constant conflicts between the country's two largest language communities, the Flemish and the francophones.

Even if these divisions should be nuanced at the level of public opinion,[2] the political system is unmistakably strongly divided. This is in part the consequence of the consociational nature of the Belgian federation.[3] It is especially visible in the party system(s), with almost all political parties represented in the federal parliament being organized at the level of only one language community, making the radical left PVDA-PTB, which has MPs elected in the Chamber of Representatives since 2014, Belgium's only national party. This lack of federal parties is one of the unique characteristics of Belgium's brand of federalism and also one of the main elements that contribute to its centrifugal nature.

The existence of two largely distinct public spheres is also an element of division: separate education systems and media landscapes lead to a situation where both Dutch and French-speakers have little knowledge of what is going on in the other language group.[4] Even though research shows that Flemish and Walloons have quite similar views on many concrete political questions, voting behavior also differs between the north of the country generally leaning more to the right and the south where (center-) left parties are more successful, a difference that is also reflected in the 2019 electoral results.[5]

The federalization of the country, through six consecutive constitutional reforms since 1970, was also largely driven by a centrifugal logic of division. Even though party political and other strategic motivations also played a role,[6] one of the main ideas behind the process was that matters on which Flemish and francophone politicians disagreed would be more efficiently handled at the sub-state level.[7] This type of argument was very often used when transfers of competences were debated in the past and it continues to be used to explain the necessity of a seventh state reform.

On top of all this, Belgium was in the middle of a political crisis when the pandemic appeared. In March 2020, Belgium had a minority caretaker government at the federal level, composed of the Dutch- and French-speaking liberal parties (Open VLD and MR) and the Flemish Christian-democrats (CD&V), who together held only 38 out of 150 seats in the Chamber. This was already the case since December 2018 when the government headed by prime minister Charles Michel fell over the UN migration pact.[8] In October 2019, after Charles Michel was appointed to become the next President of the European Council, Sophie Wilmès—a francophone liberal who hadn't been directly elected in the previous federal election of 2014 and only joined the Michel government in 2015 in replacement of another francophone liberal minister who had resigned—was appointed to temporarily act as prime minister of the caretaker government.

After the federal elections of 26 May 2019, it had not been possible to form a new government. When the corona crisis hit, the latest pair of politicians who had received a mission by the King to form a new government was in place: the presidents of the Chamber and Senate. One of the problems in the negotiations was the impossibility to unite the largest Flemish party, the Flemish nationalist N-VA, and the largest francophone party, the social-democratic PS, in one government, while the presence of N-VA was a condition for some other Flemish parties to participate in a government and the PS was necessary for almost any potential coalition. Also, almost all parties that were involved in the government formation process were to some extent in crisis as they had strongly lost the elections, with only the radical right and radical left parties and to a lesser extent the greens having gained votes.

In the meantime, regional and community governments had been formed, even if most of these formations also took longer than normal: on the Flemish level, the center-right coalition lead by N-VA was reconducted, the Walloon and French-speaking community governments became an alliance of socialists, liberals and greens while the Brussels regional government was composed of the socialist family, the green family, the Flemish liberals and the Brussels francophone party Défi.

Mid-March 2020, a new attempt was made to unite N-VA and PS and quickly form a new government, as some saw the pressure of the corona crisis as a means to finally force such an alliance. However, this didn't work out, resulting in an agreement to keep the minority caretaker government in place. It received the confidence of a large majority in parliament, legally becoming a government with full powers, which however politically engaged itself before parliament to only exercise those full powers to fight the corona crisis. To do this, it also received special powers from the parliament, allowing it to make decisions without having to go through a parliamentary vote first. Prime minister Wilmès suddenly saw herself at the head of a government with full powers, having to deal with (one of) the largest crisis since World War II.

In May, when the most urgent phase of the crisis seemed to be over, attempts at forming a new federal government were revived. During the summer, a basic agreement between N-VA and PS finally occurred, but the two parties failed to convince the two liberal parties who had presented themselves as undividable and were necessary for a parliamentary majority to agree to their project. This only left the option of a coalition of Flemish and Francophone socialists, liberals, greens, and Flemish Christian-democrats. While having gradually and somewhat reluctantly developed an identity as a federal governing party in the previous legislature,[9] the N-VA was left in the federal opposition. The Flemish liberal Alexander De Croo—who was one of the vice prime ministers in the Wilmès government—became Belgium's new prime minister.

So when the second wave arrived, Belgium did have a new, fully-fledged federal government which could be expected to give a stronger response to the health care crisis. However, it had a largely different composition than the Flemish government, again a recipe for conflicts and obstructions, as the recent past had already shown.[10] Especially the fact that the Flemish-nationalist N-VA would from then on become the main opposition party at the federal level whilst leading the Flemish government promised to create tensions. A Flemish sub-state level led by a party that has Flemish autonomy as its core business could not be expected to contribute to a unified Belgian response, especially at a time when the combined electoral score of Flemish-nationalist parties was one of the highest in Belgian history.

The confrontation with a major crisis could therefore certainly be expected to exacerbate the divided federal logic and lead to a very fragmented policy response, interlaced with territorial conflicts and coordination problems between the different government levels as has been the case in many other multinational and/or federal countries like Germany, the UK, Spain, the US, etc.[11] A country like Germany, which can hardly be considered as multi-national and which has a federal system regarded as very stable, regularly had issues that one would typically expect in Belgium, such as sometimes absurd differences between Länder during the first wave and severe difficulties of coordination and outright conflicts between political leaders at the national and sub-state levels. So, if other federal countries were somewhat unexpectedly starting to act "Belgian," it could be expected of the Belgian system with its structurally ingrained divisions and faced with a context of political crisis to go into overdrive. Especially since crisis moments can cause critical junctures for (multinational) states.[12]

A surprisingly uniform and national response

Given the context of a structurally divided country amidst a political crisis, Belgium's handling of the crisis can however be considered as surprisingly "national." Indeed, during most of the period, there was a large consensus that the COVID-19 measures should be taken in a uniform way for the entire country. Even when entirely devolved competences were concerned, such as education and culture, most measures were in application for the entire Belgian territory. The crisis can therefore be considered as having an effect toward centralization and cooperation.[13] This can be seen in the organization of the decision-making bodies, in the COVID-19 policies these produced as well as in the communication of these policies.

Federal decision-making bodies

First of all, Belgium's divided structures were quickly oriented toward the ability to generate a quite unified response. From the start of the pandemic in March 2020, a need for a stronger and more broadly supported federal government was felt. A large majority supported the attribution of full powers to the minority caretaker government for six months through a confidence vote, as well as the attribution of special powers to this now fully-fledged Wilmès government, which permitted it to act without the support of parliament, thus saving precious time. This alliance was initially called the "great union." Only the radical left PVDA/PTB and the radical right Vlaams Belang voted against in both cases. The N-VA was more nuanced but clearly also more hesitant as to which position to take. For a radical Flemish-nationalist party, it was indeed not easy to determine its position in the context of a broadly felt need for strong federal governance in crisis time: the party did not want to give the impression that it was blocking the federal government's ability to act strongly, but it did also not want to create the perception that it would give full support to an incumbent government that it had left only a bit more than a year before. So, it did not vote in favor of granting the Wilmès government the confidence to act as a government with full powers, but it did however support the attribution of special powers so that the government would not have to pass through parliament. Within the framework of this last choice, the N-VA again showed a double face. While the presidents of the ten concerned parties were supposed to weekly meet with the government to follow up on corona policies, N-VA president Bart De Wever decided to not participate and sent the leader of the N-VA's party group in parliament to weekly discuss with the nine other party presidents. This coming together of all party leaders contributed to creating crisis management in which the typically trenchant party divides were bridged.[14]

More important than the federal government as such for Belgium's response to the pandemic threat was the forum that united all six governments in the country. Indeed, since the very beginning of the crisis, it was considered necessary that the main leaders of Belgium's six governments had to make decisions on corona measures together, clearly reflecting a consensus for a common, national approach. In the period of the Wilmès government—March to October 2020—this happened through the National Security Council (NSC) which became one of the most important decision-making bodies during the COVID-19 crisis. Created in 2015 by the center-right government of Charles Michel to take measures concerning terrorist threats, it was initially composed of only federal representatives: the prime minister, the minister of justice, the minister of defense, the minister of interior affairs, the minister of foreign affairs and the vice prime ministers and representatives of security services. For the COVID-19 crisis, it was extended to the five minister-presidents of the regions and communities. They always flanked federal prime minister Sophie Wilmès during press conferences that followed the meetings of the NSC where all measures were communicated to the general public.

When the new federal De Croo government was formed in October 2020, the main decision-making body became the Concertation Committee (CC). This political organ is part of Belgium's federal system, containing representatives of the different governments in Belgium with the aim of avoiding or settling conflicts of interests between the different government levels through "concertation." It is composed in "double parity": there are as many Dutch-speakers as French-speakers and as many representatives of the federal government as representatives of the governments of the regions and communities. It can only decide through consensus. In the past, the CC prepared the NSC. Although both organs have quite different roles, for the handling of the corona crisis the difference was in practice quite minimal, since the same actors are more or less represented. However, a difference is that the CC is purely a political organ whereas for the NSC experts could also be invited. The CC was seen as an easier and more effective way to decide about new measures, especially since there were more press leaks through the NSC. Also, the regions were happier with the CC since it allowed a clearer and more official representation of the regions. This fitted in a broad strategy of the De Croo government to have more institutional participation of the regions and communities in the decision-making process (see below).

During the entire period, the measures decided by the NSC and the CC were judicially translated into law by ministerial decrees, taken by the federal minister of interior affairs. This way federal norms imposed drastic measures concerning competences of the regions and communities, such as the closing of schools, but also far-reaching suspensions of individual freedoms and constitutional rights. The legal ground for this was regularly put into question, especially through procedures before the Council of State, which however largely legitimated this way of functioning.[15]

As in most other countries, experts played a crucial role in advising the governments and preparing decisions of the NSC. Different new bodies composed of experts were created during the crisis. Gradually, criticism grew on what some considered to be a too large influence of experts, who also used their enormous media exposure—especially in Flemish audiovisual media who have more news and current affair formats—to advocate more strict measures that politicians were sometimes reluctant to take. The daily public communication of the COVID-19 state of affairs and measures was also largely in the hands of virologists and epidemiologists, especially during the Wilmès period. This "depoliticization" of communication has initially probably contributed to a very broad public acceptance of COVID-19 measures. Some associated this "depoliticization" with the limited credibility the current government had as a mere "placeholder" government and criticized the government for trying to "hide" behind the scientists. When the De Croo government took over, its members also to some extent took over TV and radio studios from medical experts.

Uniform policies

The choice to set up and/or reinforce common decision-making bodies reflected a surprising consensus that uniform national COVID-19 measures should be decided, which has throughout the crisis indeed largely been the case, in contrary to many other federal and/or multinational states. This didn't mean that there weren't any differences in policy choices between the different governments but what is probably even more surprising is that when these occurred, the typical Belgian solution to just differentiate policies was not applied, even on competences that belong to the domain of the regions and communities.

For instance, at the start of the pandemic in March 2020, most Francophone parties were pushing for the closing of schools (especially after France had taken a similar decision) while Flemish parties wanted to keep them open. It was not decided that every community could decide on its own–the typical Belgian reaction to differences in policy preferences—but a compromise was sought and found within the National Security Council. Even a Flemish government lead by Flemish-nationalists inscribed itself in the search to largely implement the same measures throughout the Belgian territory.

Another example of unexpected uniformity can be found within the culture sector. Culture has been a competence of the communities ever since the first state reform of 1970 but even here a choice for uniformity of measures was made. Given the urgency of the situation it might not be such a surprise that the NSC decided to suspend all cultural activities right from the start of the first wave of corona infections in March. But also at the time of the easing of the measures, mid-May and July, the communities still decided to inscribe themselves in national measures. As such, cultural activities were allowed again in a minimal form, starting on the first of July for a public of maximum 200 persons. Protocols with common guidelines, to make sure that everything would open smoothly, were jointly written by the three community ministers of Culture. The rationale was that this would prevent public confusion. At the time, Flemish minister-president Jambon even declared it would be absurd to have different rules for theaters in Antwerp, Brussels and Liège. Only in October there was a more fundamental but very short lived difference (see below). So, whilst the communities had the competences to draft their own rules and measures for the cultural sector, they in the end always opted for cooperation and even centralization.

A uniform response even occurred in a domain that was explicitly attributed to the sub-state levels: contact-tracing. Although there first had been confusion and discussion between the health care ministers in the interministerial committee, it was, in the end, decided that contact-tracing should be executed by the communities. The federal government provided a legal framework and supported the communities to speed up their roll-out of contact-tracing. At first, it was expected that the communities would opt for different ways to organize this, certainly given the strong autonomist preferences that live within the Flemish government. However, this was not the case. At first the Flemish Minister of Wellbeing Wouter Beke—from the Christian-democratic party CD&V—investigated whether consultancy firms could help in the roll-out of a performant contact-tracing system. However, all kinds of administrative and other problems came in the way. When it became clear that the French community and the Brussels Common Community Commission were looking in the direction of the health insurance funds for the rollout, Minister Beke also started investigating this track. In the end, the communities ended up with the same system in which the health funds played a decisive role. Moreover, the health funds even divided the task neatly between them. In the best-pillarized tradition that had marked Belgian politics and society for most of the previous century, the Christian health fund operated in Flanders, the socialist one in Wallonia, and the liberal one in Brussels. Again, this uniform approach is remarkable in a multinational state as Belgium, as the sub-states clearly had the opportunity to mark their own policy.

In the end, there were only a few clear exceptions to the rule of Belgian uniformity. The most important one is undoubtedly the variation that occurred in curfew times. Although these initially also varied between provinces, during most of the second wave their were regional variations. While initially, the Flemish region had a later curfew than Wallonia and Brussels, in the end the Walloon government aligned itself on the Flemish situation, leaving only Brussels with a stricter regime before the curfew was lifted altogether in the entire country.

A national communication

Uniform policies produced by common decision-making bodies also contributed to making the communication of the COVID-19 measures very "national." Since the measures were almost all applicable to the entire Belgian territory, the communication was clearly aimed at all Belgians, which was therefore unavoidably addressed as one nation, reinforcing the construction of a Belgian "imagined community."[16] While banal nationalism in Belgium is generally often Flemish or francophone, the pandemic clearly lead to forms of Belgian banal nationalism.[17] Also, the communication was often dominated by the federal government, with the five regional and community governments on the side.

In the first phase when decisions were taken by the NSC and communicated at press conferences where the leaders of all governments were present, the main communication was generally left to federal prime minister Wilmès. Only on one occasion in this period, the five other minister-presidents also took the floor. Wilmès' communication was regularly met with criticism. However, again at odds with what one might expect in a divided country where sub-state autonomy is declared sacred, Wilmès was not criticized for a too centralist and national communication, taking all the place and leaving the regional and community governments in her shadow. On the contrary, she was often pilloried for not showing herself as a strong national leader. Indeed, some compared her talks at press conferences with the "speeches to the nation" held by heads of states in neighboring countries and found that Wilmès was communicating too blandly, expecting her to act more states(wo)manlike, such as the French president Emmanuel Macron or the German Chancellor Angela Merkel. Ironically, these critiques and expectations also came from more regionalist politicians and opinion-makers. Moreover, the press conference during the first wave where all minister-presidents spoke was also criticized partly for this very reason, as commentators found that this further contributed to taking the dynamic out of the Belgian authorities' communication. In reaction, Wilmès did indeed try to address "the nation" in a more empathic way, also in one instance with a personal but also "presidential"-like video message.

When the new De Croo government came to power, a communication shift was noticeable on different levels. The federal government explicitly gave a place to the minister-presidents of the regions and communities during press conferences. The federal level communicated more about the general measures, whereas the minister-presidents focused on specific details concerning regional and community competences. This can be explained due to the shift from the NSC to the CC, which allowed the sub state governments to be more visible. This could be considered as quite ironic, given the fact that the new federal government was much more legitimate than the boosted minority caretaker government it had replaced. However, simultaneously, the federal coalition's own communication was strengthened, making also the overall communication strongly centered around Prime Minister De Croo and federal Health Minister Frank

Vandenbroucke, who were both addressing the general public more frequently and strongly than their predecessors. The new government's active media presence made it more visible than its predecessor in the fight against corona: while at the time of the Wilmès government, communication was often left to the experts, ministers of the new federal government were more eager to take their place. These were however mostly Dutch-speaking ministers, as they largely held the portfolios primarily concerned with the pandemic: next to De Croo and Vandenbroucke—a Flemish liberal and a Flemish socialist—also the minister of interior affairs belonged to a Flemish party, the Christian-democratic one. This did create at times some frustration among francophone parties in the federal government and especially among the francophone liberal party which regularly criticized a number of the COVID measures that were decided, even though the party did have three representatives in the CC.

Debates on the nature of the demos and the nation were also conducted more explicitly, as the De Croo government launched a campaign playing into and at the same time also reinforcing a national Belgian feeling that comes with handling the pandemic. The idea behind this campaign called "A team of 11 million" was that all Belgians form one team, a unity needed to beat the virus. It was conducted on TV, radio, print media and social media. People were also invited to hang posters on their windows. On Christmas Eve, in the framework of the campaign, a TV show was broadcast on public and private broadcasting channels across the language border. That all channels broadcasted a common program was a unique event in Belgium's strongly linguistically fragmented media landscape. The campaign, in general, was quite a novel initiative in the Belgian context, as these kinds of "nation building" efforts are generally only conducted by governments at the sub-state levels, and especially by the Flemish government. It can therefore come as no surprise that the federal campaign was not appreciated by Flemish nationalists, who accused the federal government of instrumentalizing the health crisis and spending more than three million euros for a political project of Belgian unity and patriotism. Additionally, they were cynical about the idea of a "team," given that the current government parties needed such a long time to form a government. Vlaams Belang claimed that this campaign used an artificial feeling to invoke an artificial country. Nevertheless, the Flemish-nationalist radical party, while sometimes opposing the content of COVID-policies, didn't fundamentally criticize the uniform national nature of the measures.

Drivers toward national uniformity

The question is how we can explain this quite paradoxical situation where divided Belgium opted for a largely uniform national response.

One of the explanations lies in Belgium's unique division of sub-state competences over two overlapping types of federated entities, the regions and communities, and more specifically in its consequences for the Brussels region where the two large communities are also competent. Therefore, different policies on community competences such as education, culture, and sports in Brussels is, therefore, a normal situation Belgian policymakers have become accustomed to. However, it seems that in times of crisis, this way of operating is considered far from ideal. Indeed, if different measures would be taken on community competences, this would therefore mean two different COVID-regimes on the territory of the Brussels region.

For instance, if the Flemish community would decide to leave schools open while the French-speaking community would close them, the situation for schools on the Brussels territory would be strongly different depending on the community they fall under: in a specific street, one school would be allowed to open while the other might be forced to close, leading to incomprehension and confusion for many parents and children. The same is true for the cultural sector. That the Brussels situation indeed played a role was shown when the communities needed to write protocols in order to reopen the cultural sector. In August, the French community decided to have a 1-m distance rule between "bubbles" at cultural events instead of the initially foreseen 1.5 m to which the Flemish community initially stuck. This difference was strongly criticized by representatives of the cultural sector in Brussels who complained that this would create discrimination between theaters in Brussels, Flemish theaters not being able to receive as many spectators than francophone ones. The Flemish community then quite quickly decided to align itself to the 1-m rule. Also, in the field of sports activities, another competence of the communities, the measures were synchronized to prevent strange situations in Brussels, such as the rule during the second wave that only people under 12 years old were allowed to play sport in a team, whereas people older than 12 were not. One can only imagine that this would lead to situations perceived by many as bizarre and surreal if such synchronization was absent.

This is especially true in the broader context of the current debate on Belgium's federalism and Brussels' place in it. Indeed, in recent years the idea that Brussels is in large part the sum of the two large language communities who cohabit there—an idea on which the federal architecture was based—is considered more than ever at odds with the socio-demographic reality of a multilingual and diverse metropolitan area. More broadly, discussions in preparation of a possible seventh state reform focus on the possibility of leaving the double federal model with regions and communities to replace it by a model based on four territorial sub-states, which would in theory make the Brussels region competent for the current community competences on its territory. The sixth state reform has already put some small steps in this direction.[18]

One could say that the logic of this model of a "Belgium with four" has already been followed for Brussels during the pandemic, even though the Brussels uniformity is of course only part of a more general federal uniformity, of which it can be considered one of the drivers. However, at one point this Brussels regional logic became very visible. This was during the only and short period in October 2020 when no consensus could be found in the CC on stricter national corona measures concerning community competences such as culture (for more details, see below). The governments of the Walloon Region and the French community announced additional measures, which were however only imposed in the Walloon region. One day later, the Brussels regional government announced partly different measures for its territory: while museums and (movie) theaters remained open in the Flemish and Walloon region (but had to close earlier due to the curfew), they were closed in the Brussels region. Thus, the Brussels regional government took measures related to competences that it does not possess, in what could be seen as foreshadowing a new model of a "Belgium with four" where the

Brussels region would also gain community competences. In the chaos that followed the lack of national consensus, community competences were de facto regionalized for a few days.

Another explanation for the uniform national handling of the COVID-19 crisis is that amid a health crisis in which every decision and its impact is strongly scrutinized and also potentially criticized, the different governments were afraid to use their autonomy to take separate measures which might, in the end, turn out worse than those taken by other governments. This dynamic is quite opposite to a classical federal logic in which it is considered that federalism creates opportunities for experimentation. Separate and diverging decisions taken by different regional governments allow for policy comparison and possibly also for policy improvement, allowing governments to explore the benefits of specific public policies.[19] Here, it seems that this federalism-as-a-laboratory approach and the consequent comparison of policies was feared by Belgian decision-makers. In any case, it seems that they did not consider that federalism would allow more flexibility, another traditional advantage ascribed to federalism. The fact that the regional governments opted for a uniform response, might indicate that they didn't have the capacity to behave (more) flexibly—a necessity in times of crisis—and opted for the "easier" response, namely a uniform one.

It also seems that regional and community governments realized that public opinion demanded a strong national response and did not want to be confronted with absurd differences in a small country in times of crisis. This indeed seems to be corroborated by public opinion research on the satisfaction with the different governments and ministers and on the distribution of competences (see further), amongst other things showing a clear public frustration over the fact that Belgium has nine ministers of health and a demand for more unity of command with a strong role for the prime minister and federal government.

Furthermore, the existence of different federal institutions managing the situation also contributed to steer the policy-makers toward national measures and to reinforce a common federal dynamic. For instance, an important role was played by Sciensano, the federal scientific institution and research center for public health which published the daily figures of new infections, hospital admittances, and deaths. Their Dutch-speaking and French-speaking spokespersons became household names, both in their own community. Sciensano also presided the RAG (Risk Assessment Group), which also contained experts from the sub-state administrations and which advised the RMG (Risk Management Group), composed of different health authorities at the different governmental levels. Most other relevant advisory bodies were also national and the De Croo government additionally appointed a federal corona commissioner, which reinforced the federal level's directive role (see also below). More generally, virologists and epidemiologists, continuously had a very important say on COVID-policies, also because they were very present in the media and their support among public opinion was very high. A study by news magazines *Knack* and *Le Vif/L'Express* showed satisfaction rates for the most visible experts between 60% and 80% while the most prominent ministers only scored between 13% and 39% (Wilmes having the best score). While most experts were not really nationally visible–as Flemish and francophone media mostly gave the floor to experts of their own language community—most of them structurally strived for measures that applied to the entire territory, amongst other reasons because they believed this would be the clearest for the population, leading to better follow-up.

In a divided federal country like Belgium, there are of course also strong drivers toward more regionalist dynamics, such as the regional governments and especially the Flemish government. However, in this crisis they were not able to affect the more national dynamic.

Flemish nationalism caught between a rock and a hard place

In theory, the pandemic presented an ideal opportunity for sub-state levels to acquire and show leadership and credibility in a multi-national context, which could only help in strengthening the autonomist project. Normally, regional levels can also take credit for well-executed policies and shift the blame to the national governments if something goes wrong.[20] However, the accounts above show that, despite having several leverages at its disposal, the Flemish government led by the Flemish-nationalist N-VA never used these to a full extent and was not able to leave its mark in the handling of the pandemic, not even when the federal level was governed by a minority government.

While the N-VA had in recent years showed itself to be quite flexible in adapting its discourse and positions to a changing political context,[21] it initially had difficulties positioning itself toward this new problem. At the very beginning of the pandemic, the party's leader and mayor of Antwerp Bart De Wever went in one week from questioning the need for strict measures to criticizing the federal government for not taking very stringent measures. After the formation of the federal De Croo government, N-VA struggled even more to navigate between being an opposition party at the federal level and leading the Flemish government. While their Flemish minister-president Jan Jambon decided on all COVID-19 measures in consensus with other government leaders within the CC, other N-VA representatives were at different times quite critical in attempts at blame-shifting to the federal level. The leader of the N-VA group in the federal Chamber put into question the legitimacy of the federal government by becoming one of the most vocal political critics of the unconstitutional way the COVID-19 measures were adapted: through "ministerial decisions" largely leaving the parliament outside. According to him, a "pandemic law" should be adopted that stipulates what the government can and cannot do to combat the (next) pandemic, with a more important role for parliament. However, this attitude was criticized by other parties, who remarked that at the Flemish level the parliament was not really involved by the government either. This position at the federal level could be considered a logical consequence of N-VA's opposition status there, but at different times Flemish ministers part of the government lead by their party colleague Jambon also attacked decisions he had contributed to take. For instance, in October the Flemish minister of Tourism criticized the decision of the CC to close the bars and restaurants. And in March 2021, the Flemish minister of education vehemently criticized the decision to close the schools the week before Easter.

Flemish minister-president Jambon at moments also clearly struggled in finding a balance between trying to profile the Flemish sub state level in the handling of the crisis—often by publicly resisting stricter measures or pleading for more relaxations—and his role in the CC where consensus had to be found. One episode in October 2020 is particularly relevant in this respect, as it is the only time where centralizing instincts of the federal government were fundamentally opposed by the Flemish government and the logic of a uniform policy response was endangered. The CC was not able to find a consensus on stricter measures in the education, sports and cultural sectors proposed by experts and largely supported by the federal level and other sub state governments as Jambon opposed these. A day later the governments of the Walloon region and the French community therefore implemented more or less the measures originally on the CC-table, followed by the Brussels government with even stricter measures, leaving behind the Flemish government.

As argument for his resistance, Jambon referred to the specific situation in Flanders. Indeed, this was the only period when infection rates differed, as they were much higher in the Walloon and Brussels regions than in the Flemish region. However, experts argued that Flanders was only a week behind in a very similar evolution so that it would quickly face the same rising infection rates if it didn't act immediately. What initially seemed to some as the Flemish government finally claiming its autonomy and giving Flanders a different COVID policy, very quickly backfired. Jambon was heavily criticized for not understanding epidemiological logics. Also, many agreed that it was chaotic to have varying measures per region. Under the pressure of experts, opposition parties and rising corona infections the Flemish government saw itself forced to announce about the same measures as those in place in Brussels and Wallonia, only five days after it had blocked these measures in the CC. Quickly, prime minister De Croo called for a new CC resulting in a federal ministerial decree which synchronized the measures. The only difference that remained was a curfew time that was two hours later in the Flemish region than the rest of the country. The solo-slim of the Flemish government was heavily criticized. In that way, rather than announcing a new dynamic where the national uniform COVID-response would be replaced by varying regional policies, the Flemish government's attempt at reinforcing its autonomy rather convinced many that regional variation created chaos and thus reinforced the national unified dynamic.

N-VA's Flemish minister of education Ben Weyts also had an outspoken position on keeping the schools open as much as possible. This created some minimal differences with the French-speaking community during the first wave (such as Flemish schools having one "trial day" before officially reopening on the same date as French-speaking schools), while in the later stages it lead to clear conflicts with the federal minister of health. In March, Vandenbroucke wanted to close the schools a week before the Easter holidays would start, something that both communities strongly opposed, but which was in the end adopted by the CC. A hard pill to swallow for Weyts who openly criticized the decision of the CC, also agreed on by his party colleague and Minister President Jan Jambon, who was again perceived not to weigh on policies. In any case, Jambon did not want to seem to repeat his "experiment" of October by blocking the national school closure. A little later, Jambon did still suggest that if the degree of vaccination would remain structurally higher among the Flemish population, Flanders should be able to relax rules more quickly than the rest of the country, but this was never an option that was seriously considered by experts or within the CC.

In the meantime, taking credit for well-executed policies was not easy for the Flemish government as it was generally not able to create an image of efficient leadership and competent management in the fight against the virus. For instance, at the early stages of the pandemic, Flemish minister of Wellbeing Wouter Beke was strongly attacked for his handling of the situation in the residential care centers, which was quickly referred to as a "drama." Nursing staff complained about the lack of testing material, protective material and support, leading to many deaths that could be avoided. The contact-tracing system was also regularly criticized for a fundamental lack of efficiency and transparency. While the situation was not necessarily better in the south of the country, on the Flemish side it was clearly at odds with the image of efficiency that Flemish governments generally try to propagate. Only when the vaccination campaign started to run smoothly with high numbers of vaccinated people, the Flemish minister of well-being had an argument to build on.

The effect of this weak response seems to be reflected in public opinion studies. At the beginning of the COVID-19 crisis, the federal government seems to have witnessed a short "rally around the flag effect," with a temporary higher peak of satisfaction which the Flemish government didn't reach. Satisfaction ratings of Belgian Prime Minister Wilmès were, at the beginning of April 2020, over 50%, although they strongly dropped during the month, while Jambon only left a good impression on some 30% of the Flemish population. Later, satisfaction in Flanders with the Flemish government (40%) was similar to that with the federal government (41%), which had often been criticized because of its minority status. Moreover, 7 out of 10 Flemish respondents agreed that the minority caretaker government was at that time the best way to deal with the pandemic.[22] A follow-up study one year later showed that satisfaction with both governments' COVID response had dropped but that the federal government (28%) scored better than the Flemish government (23%). The difference was more striking when individual ministers' COVID policies are compared: federal prime minister De Croo had left a much better impression on Flemish respondents than Flemish minister-president Jambon (49% vs 22%). Also, the different federal ministers scored better (between 32% and 49%) than their Flemish counterparts (between 11% and 25%).[23]

However, the popularity of the federal ministers does not seem to transfer to their parties, as in voting polls Flemish-nationalist parties remain clearly more popular, with N-VA and Vlaams Belang regularly reaching close to half of the total voting intentions (with N-VA losing ground to VB though). So while the Corona crisis rather weakened then strengthened Flemish-nationalist ideals when the response of the different government levels is compared, it does not seem to have affected Flemish-nationalists' electoral potential. This does not have to be too surprising as studies show that Flemish-nationalist positions on state reform are not the main motivation of the electorate of N-VA and Vlaams Belang.[24] And while the surprisingly uniform Belgian handling of the crisis together with the weak performance of the Flemish government could also be considered as hampering Flemish-nationalists in their hopes for further constitutional reform, they can still focus on the problems that occurred in the execution of these policies.

A national policy response executed with fragmented competencies

While as described above, the COVID-19 policy response in Belgium was largely uniformally national in terms of measures taken, to some extent defying the conflictual and centrifugal dynamics ingrained in Belgium's federal system, this system did shape and hamper the execution in the back office where the very fragmented and complex division of competences regularly created problems.

Some of the health competences were already attributed to the communities during the second state reform in 1980. The communities became responsible for prevention, homecare, some parts of the first line healthcare, elderly health care, and hospitals. This didn't change much until the sixth state reform of 2012, when additional competences were devolved to the communities, such as psychiatric nursing homes, the financing of elderly care, and revalidation hospitals. Moreover, the financing of the building, renovation, equipment, and the furniture of hospitals were also devolved. In some sectors, the competences were harmonized, such as in care for the disabled, elderly care, and mental health care. For instance, before the sixth state reform the purchase of a wheelchair was paid by the federal health insurance while the repair and maintenance of the same wheelchair was paid by the communities. However, this doesn't mean that the sixth reform created homogenous competences. For example, the organization of first-line health care and residential care centers became a competence for the communities but the financing of home nursing and the payment of the family doctor remained a federal competence. Also, for the hospitals, the financing remained largely a federal competence.[25] As becomes clear, health care competences are distributed in a very complex and fragmented way.

Because health care is that divided between the federal level and the federated entities, the Interministerial Committee (ICM) for Health Care is an important body, as it is responsible for the coordination of health care policies of the different authorities and composed of all members of the different governments that are competent for health care. During the corona crisis, nine ministers were officially competent. First of all, there is the federal minister of health care. Since the communities are competent for other aspects, there are also the three community ministers (Flemish, French-speaking, and Dutch-Speaking). This competence of the communities also implies that two ministers are competent in Brussels (one for the Flemish and one for the French-speaking Community Commission and both for the Common Community Commission), which makes six. Some competences have however also been attributed to the regions, which adds a minister from the Walloon region (the Flemish region and community have been merged under one government and parliament). The two final ministers result from the fact that within the Walloon government and the French-speaking community Commission competences on health care have this legislature been divided over two ministers at the time of government formation.

So, nine ministers are competent but only eight of them are actual members of the IMC since it was decided that the minister of the French-speaking Community Commission in Brussels would also represent his colleague, minister in that same commission. Actually, the minister of the Flemish Community Commission is officially a member but is in practice also represented at the meetings of the IMC by her colleague of the French community commission. The fact that all three belong to the same political "family"—the greens—which is also the family with the closest ties between the Flemish and French-speaking party, especially in Brussels, explains why the Brussels representatives were able to "simplify" their representation. So the IMC counts eight ministers from seven different political parties. During the first wave, a federal minister who was made responsible for increasing the testing capacity and ordering medical protection material was also added.

The reports of the meetings of the IMC during the COVID-19 crisis show that the efficiency of decision-making was hampered by the complex distribution of competences. For instance, it was unclear for a long-time which authority was exactly competent for contact tracing, the communities or the federal level, which eventually lead to public conflicts between the Flemish minister and a federal minister and a delayed startup. The orders of protection material were often carried out separately by the different authorities, without much coordination or even transparency, also leading to inefficiency. There were also coordination problems with the Risk Management Group (RMG), although the latter is composed of representatives of the cabinets of the different ministers competent for health, which lead amongst other things to delays in developing a clear testing strategy. The fact that eight (or nine) ministers were competent for health care became a very illustrative symbol for many people of the problematic organization of health care within Belgium. In a television interview, when asked to name the eight ministers, prime minister De Croo had to admit that he couldn't. The appointment of a corona commissioner by the new federal De Croo government was also meant to ensure better coordination between the federal government and the federated entities and thus improve decision-making.

The problems of collaboration and coordination between the different levels of government competent for health care reinforced a large consensus that the current distribution of competences is strongly problematic. However, parties differ on the solution: Flemish nationalists somewhat ironically strongly criticize the number of health ministers in Belgium but obviously see it as an argument to only have one minister for Flanders. A further defederalization of health care is also a priority for Flemish Christian-democrats, as this would reinforce the catholic pillar which still strongly dominates the Flemish health sector. Many leading figures in the sector also have close ties to CD&V. Since the first competences on health care were devolved in 1980, the Flemish minister of well-being and health care has always been a Christian-democrat, with the exception for the one term when the party was in opposition. At the same time, Flemish and Francophone liberals and greens tend to plead for a refederalisation of competences now devolved to the federated entities. Studies among Belgian MPs show growing support for the principle of refederalisation, especially among green, liberal, but also socialist representatives.[26] This support is also present in part of the health care sector and especially among public opinion: a survey by Roularta Media Group showed that 85% of the Belgian hospital directors think that health care should be organized at the federal level, while one conducted by VTM Nieuws, HLN, RTL and Le Soir among the population at large indicated that 86% of respondents thought that nine ministers of Health care is "senseless." When these were asked which government level should then become competent, 71% chose the federal level.

However, during the formation of the De Croo government, it seems the Flemish Christian-democrats—for which this was a crucial condition to join the new federal coalition—managed to push through their vision, as the government agreement suggests that health care should be further defederalized. Also, the failed attempt in the summer of 2020 to form a coalition around N-VA and PS did produce a preliminary deal between the two parties which suggests that they can find a consensus on further strengthening sub state autonomy. Still, fundamental discussions, let alone negotiations, on a seventh state reform still have to start and at least eight parties will be necessary to reach an overall two-thirds majority and a simple majority in both language groups needed to adopt a new constitutional reform.

Conclusion

Since 1970, Belgium has been in a perpetuum mobile of constitutional reform, having resulted in six state reforms to date. It always starts with the observation that the system has become too complex, costly, and inefficient. The presented solution to this is then a new state reform. When this is finally realized, often after years of political instability and/or crisis, it is observed that it has made the system even more complex, costly, and inefficient, to which the solution is yet another reform. And so on. The character of this perpetuum mobile has up until now been exclusively centrifugal, all of these six state reforms having always split up more competences.

Belgian political elites are now slowly but surely preparing themselves for another round in this process. A question is whether Belgium's experiences with handling the COVID-19 crisis will play a role in this. The crisis brought forward severe difficulties related to the complex—and according to most concerned inefficient—distribution of competences in health care, which were in the line of expectations. At the same time, despite a very complex and divisive federal structure and an extremely difficult political context of political crisis and instability, Belgium largely managed to produce COVID-19 measures that were startingly uniform over the entire national territory. While normally the slightest hint of a difference in vision between political representatives of Belgium's two largest language groups is considered sufficient by many to separate policies, during the COVID-19 crisis there seemed to be a consensus among the entire political spectrum that it was necessary to provide a common, uniform national response, which was visible in the structures used to produce corona policies, in the policies themselves, in their translation to law as well as in the communication about them. Most of the time, even a Flemish government lead by a Flemish-nationalist party inscribed itself in this consensus.

The realization that strongly divergent regional measures would have created serious problems within and around Brussels and would have hampered the adhesion of the population which expected unity of command were some of the reasons for this. There seemed to be a realization that in crisis time, regional and community autonomy had to take a back seat to the need for a common coherent response at the national level. It's as if a divided and complex structure is considered acceptable in normal times when people are not paying too much attention or can laugh away some of the absurdities resulting from it, but not when things really get serious and the Belgian population expects all politicians in the country to get their act together.

This also means it is quite uncertain that there will be any long term structural consequences of the COVID response on Belgium's day to day federal and party political dynamics when the country returns to normal political life. The pressure that all politicians around the table of a Concertation Committee feel to not leave it without a consensus to present to a population in disarray will probably disappear when issues perceived as less urgent and vital have to be dealt with. For such issues, the need for a common national response is likely not to be felt at altogether.

Nevertheless, the COVID-19 crisis can leave traces on Belgium's constitutional reform debate. Since a de facto centralization has occurred to fight the pandemic, the question has been raised whether a form of hierarchy in times of crisis—possibly also of a different nature—should not be more structurally introduced in the constitution. This would be a small revolution in Belgium's federal system which was always built on the clear absence of any hierarchy between the federal and sub state government levels. It contributes to a novel dynamic that has developed in recent years where part of the intellectual and political world shows a growing concern for reinforcing federal cohesion, including openness to refederalisation of some competences. However, the question is whether parties that follow this line of thinking really consider it a priority in negotiations, while it is already clear that those who plead for further devolution do. Therefore, the question remains whether a tendency toward more centralization will find any form of translation in constitutional reform.

Notes

1. Kris Deschouwer, *The Politics of Belgium: Governing a Divided Society*, 2nd ed. (Cham: Palgrave Macmillan, 2012); Arend Lijphart, *Patterns of Democracy* (Yale: Yale University Press, 2012); Patricia Popelier, Dave Sinardet, Jan Velaers, and Bea Cantillon, *België, Quo Vadis? Waarheen na de zesde staatshervorming* (Antwerp/Cambridge: Intersentia, 2012); Mike Medeiros, Jean-Philippe Gauvin, and Chris Chhim, "Unified Voters in a Divided Society: Ideology and Regionalism in Belgium," *Regional & Federal Studies* (2020): 1–19. DOI: 10.1080/13597566.2020.1843021; Patricia Popelier, "Power-Sharing in Belgium: The Disintegrative Model," in *Power-Sharing in Europe. Past Practice, Present Cases, and Future Directions*, edited by Soeren Keil and Allison McCulloch (Cham: Palgrave Macmillan, 2021).
2. Dave Sinardet, Lieven De Winter, Jérémy Dodeigne, and Min Reuchamps, "Language Identity and Voting," in *Mind the Gap: Political Participation and Representation in Belgium*, edited by Kris Deschouwer (Colchester: ECPR Press, 2018), 113–32.
3. Dave Sinardet, "From Consociational Consciousness to Majoritarian Myth: Consociational Democracy, Multi-Level Politics and the Belgian Case of Brussels-Halle-Vilvoorde," *Acta Politica* 45, no. 3 (2010): 346–69; Kris Deschouwer, *The Politics of Belgium.*
4. Jaak Billiet, Bart Maddens, and André-Paul Frognier, "Does Belgium (Still) Exist? Differences in Political Culture between Flemings and Walloons," *West European Politics* 29, no. 5 (2006): 912–32; Dave Sinardet, "Is there a Belgian Public Sphere? What the Case of a Federal Multilingual Country Can Contribute to the Debate on Transnational Public Spheres and Vice Versa," in *Multinational Federalism: Problems and Prospects*, edited by Michel Seymour and Alain-G. Gagnon (New York: Palgrave Macmillan, 2012), 172–204; Mike Medeiros et al., "Unified Voters in a Divided Society."
5. Stefaan Walgrave, Benoît Rihoux, Sofie Marien, Emilie Van Haute, and Karen Celis, *Note Based on the Represent Study: Vlaming en Walen stemden voor verschillende partijen maar verschillen minder van mening over het beleid dat ze willen* (Brussels: EOS, 2019).
6. Dave Sinardet, "Federal Reform and Party Politics: The Case of the Fifth Belgian State Reform," in *Changing Federal Constitutions: Lessons from International Comparison*, edited by Arthur Benz and Felix Kneupling (Opladen: Barbara Budrich Publishers, 2012), 135–60.
7. Kris Deschouwer, *The Politics of Belgium;* Jean-Francois, Céline Mahieu, and Caroline Sägesser, "Federalism and Decentralization in Belgium," in *The Palgrave Handbook of Decentralization in Europe*, edited by José Manuel Ruano and Marius Profiroiu (Cham:

Palgrave Macmillan, 2016), 47–75; Anna Mastromarino, "Secessionist Claims in a Federal System," in *Claims for Secession and Federalism.*

8. See also Patricia Popelier, "COVID-19 Legislation in Belgium at the Crossroads of a Political and a Health Crisis," *The Theory and Practice of Legislation* 8, no. 1–2 (2020): 131–53.

9. Dave Sinardet, "Flemish Nationalism and the Left-Right Divide. Consequences for Constitutional Politics in Belgium," in *Constituional Politics in Multinational Democracies*, edited by André Lecours, Nikola Brassard-Dion, and Guy Laforest (Montreal: McGill-Queen's University Press, 2021), 132–57.

10. Dave Sinardet, "From Consociational Consciousness."

11. Nicole Huberfeld, Sarah H. Gordon, and David K. Jones, "Federalism Complicates the Response to the COVID-19 Health and Economic Crisis: What Can Be Done?," *Journal of Health Politics, Policy and Law* 45, no. 6 (2020): 951–65; Markus Siewert, Stefan Wurster, Luca Messerschmidt, Cindy Cheng, and Tim Butte, "A German Miracle? Crisis Management During the COVID-19 Pandemic in a Multi-Level System," in *PEX Special Report: Coronavirus Outbreak, Presidents' Responses, and Institutional Consequences*, edited by Inacio Magna and Aline Burni (Rochester, NY: SSRN, 2020); Jess Sargeant, *Co-ordination and Divergence: Devolution and Coronavirus* (London: Institute for Government, 2020); Fernando Jimenez Sanchez, *The Political Management of the COVID-19 Crisis in Spain* (Budapest: Foundation Robert Schuman, 2020); Alexandra Artiles, Martin Gandur, and Amanda Driscoll, *The (Less) United States? Federalism & Decentralization in the Era of COVID-19* (PEX Executives, Presidents and Cabinet Politics, 2020).

12. Florian Bieber, "Global Nationalism in Times of the COVID-19 Pandemic," *Nationalities Papers* (2020): 1–13. DOI: 10.1017/nps.2020.35.

13. See also Patricia Popelier, "The Impact of the Covid-19 Crisis on the Federal Dynamics in Belgium," 2020, https://uacesterrpol.wordpress.com/2020/05/05/the-impact-of-the-covid-19-crisis-on-the-federal-dynamics-in-belgium/

14. Toon Van Overbeke and Diederik Stadig, "High Politics in the Low Countries: COVID-19 and the Politics of Strained Multi-Level Policy Cooperation in Belgium and The Netherlands," *European Policy Analysis* 6, no. 2 (2020): 305–17.

15. For more details see Patricia Popelier, "COVID-19 Legislation in Belgium."

16. Cf. Benedict Anderson, *Imagined Communities: Reflections on the Origin and Spread of Nationalism* (London: Verso, 1983).

17. Cf. Michael Billig, *Banal Nationalism* (London: Sage Publications, 1995).

18. Mathias El Berhoumi, Laurie Losseau, and Sébastien Van Drooghenbroeck, "Vers une Belgique à quatre? Les compétences communautaires à Bruxelles après la sixième réforme de l'État," in *De Brusselse instellingen anno 2014/Les institutions bruxelloises en 2014*, edited by Emmanuel Van Den Bossche (Bruges: Die Keure, 2017).

19. David Nice, *Federalism: The Politics of Intergovernmental Relations* (New York: St Martin's Press, 1987); Jan Erk, Edward L. Gibson, Ugo M. Amoretti, Nancy Bermeo, Alain Noël, R. Daniel Kelemen, Mikhail Filippov, Peter C. Ordeshook, Olga Shvetsova, Pradeep Chhibber, et al. "Does Federalism Really Matter?," *Comparative Politics* 39, no. 1 (2006): 103–20.

20. Nicole Huberfeld et al., "Federalism Complicates the Response"; Kent Weaver, "The Nays Have It: How Rampant Blame Generating Distorts American Policy and Politics," *Political Science Quarterly* 133, no. 2 (2018): 259–89.

21. Dave Sinardet, "Flemish Nationalism and the Left-Right Divide."

22. Jonas Lefevere and Stefaan Walgrave, *De Stemming: Onderzoek in opdracht van de VRT en De Standaard* (Antwerp/Brussels: University of Antwerp/Free University of Brussels, 2020/2021).

23. Ibid.

24. Sinardet et al., "Language Identity and Voting," in *Mind the Gap.*

25. Popelier et al., *België, Quo Vadis?*; Aube Wirtgen and Dave Sinardet, *"De gezondheidscrisis, een aanzet tot efficiënt federalisme?,"* in *Post Viraal naar een nieuw normal*, edited by M. Brengman (Antwerp: ASP/VUB Press, 2020), 57–65; Koen Algoed, *De zesde staatshervorming*

en haar impact op de overheidsfinanciën doorgelicht (Leuven: Vives Research Center for Regional Economics, 2017).

26. Jérémy Dodeigne, Christoph Niessen, Min Reuchamps, and Dave Sinardet, "The Effect of Institutional Affiliation and Career Patterns on (De)Centralization Preferences in Advanced Multi-Level States: Parliamentarians' Support for (De)Centralization in Belgium," *Publius: The Journal of Federalism* 51, no. 2 (2021): 262–82.

Trumpist Ethnonationalism and the Federal Response to the COVID-19 Crisis and Other Natural Disasters in Puerto Rico (2017–21)

Jaime Lluch

ABSTRACT

The federal political system we call the United States is both a multinational and a multiethnic state. Puerto Rico has been a peripheral part of the United States since 1898, and its inclusion in the outward edges of the U.S. state apparatus turns the U.S. into a multinational democracy, exhibiting a form of peripheral multinationalism. In recent years, the rise of Trumpism and the transformation of the Republican Party have energized those who envision an ethnonationalist view of U.S. national identity: a political momentum is strengthening, sustaining a nativist, white majority nation reaction that would revive ancestral racial and ethnic concepts of U.S. national identity. This of course is not a favorable development for the accommodation and the fair treatment of Puerto Rico within the U.S. federation and has multiple ramifications, including the foot dragging behind the Republican federal government's response to the COVID-19 crisis of 2020–21, and the other major natural disasters that have impacted the island, especially the devastation caused by Hurricane María.

Introduction

COVID-19 is the greatest global challenge since World War II. Since January 2020, some of the countries most affected by the virus are federations or federal political systems,[1] and many of these are multinational and/or multiethnic states. In this article, I examine a complex multilevel system, the United States of America, which in its core federation is a highly diverse multiethnic state, but which is also multinational if we consider it as a wider federal political system, with peripheral sub-state national societies, especially as it pertains to the "unincorporated territory" of Puerto Rico.

Seen from this perspective, the federal system we call the United States is both a multinational and a multiethnic state. Puerto Rico has been a peripheral part of the United States since the U.S.-Spanish-Cuban War of 1898, and its inclusion in the outward edges of the U.S. state apparatus turns the U.S. into a multinational democracy. Multinational democracies are constitutional polities that contain two or more nations or peoples where the members of the sub-state nation(s) may aspire to determine their own future and quotas of self-government, whether externally (via full independence) or internally (via forms of autonomism or federalism).[2] The United States may also exhibit plurinationalism to the extent that some people in Puerto Rico may hold overlapping or nested national identities.[3]

Trumpism was in power between January 2017 and January 2021. Within this same time period, Puerto Rico has been clobbered by three consecutive natural disasters: first, the devastation by Hurricanes María and Irma in 2017 which were the worst natural cataclysms in a century, then multiple earthquakes between December 2019 and late 2020, followed by the worldwide onset of the COVID-19 pandemic. This article argues that the Trump administration, which exuded a new ethnonational ideology, has been callous, sluggish, and has dragged its feet in its federal response to these consecutive crises. Moreover, Trump has personally shown disdain for Puerto Rico and Puerto Ricans, to the point that Puerto Rico has been disfavored, underserved, and shunned by the Trump administration. Trumpism is a new ethnonational "ascriptive form of Americanism" aiming to reformulate U.S. national identity, feeding an exclusionary state nationalism in the U.S., exacerbating national divides, and having a negative impact on Puerto Rico and Puerto Ricans. To construct this argument, the article first delves into the distinctiveness of Puerto Rico and Puerto Ricans when compared to other cases of multinationalism or stateless nationhood. I next analyze the United States as a multinational democracy. Then, I discuss the issue of U.S. national identity, multinationalism, and the national divide(s) that exist in the federal political system that we call the U.S. and its impact on Puerto Rico. The new ethnonationalism of Trumpism and its notions of national identity are then analyzed in view of Puerto Rico, aiming to help us understand the roots of Trumpism's disdain for Puerto Rico and its sluggishness in providing an adequate response to the multiple crises there. Following this, I discuss in detail the federal response to the COVID-19 crisis and the other natural disasters in Puerto Rico in sequence. The final section analyzes the parties and political orientations in Puerto Rico, focusing on who gained and who lost because of the multiple crises and disasters, and the impact of multiple crises on the sub-state national movement(s) and the political party system in Puerto Rico.

The distinctiveness of the Puerto Rico case

Like all the other cases of multinationalism in multilevel systems considered in this special issue, there is a sense of nationhood among some Puerto Ricans which is different from the mainstream in the U.S., and the issue of national identity is multilayered in Puerto Rico. I will show below how this intersects with the management of the COVID-19 pandemic and other natural disasters.[4] However, it should be stated at the outset that in other key variables Puerto Rico is significantly different from the other cases examined in this special issue. First, the asymmetry in size, power, and wealth between the substate national society that is Puerto Rico and the majority nation that we may denominate as the United States is enormous. Second, Puerto Ricans are circulators in that they are constantly going back and forth between the continental United States and the island.[5] They are a nation that is both on the island and on the continent simultaneously, yet when they are on the continent they immediately become a racial/ethnic minority. Those communities are seen by the majority group as a racialized minority, and our discussion below will incorporate the subtleties of this national duality.[6]

Third, Puerto Rico is a case of subordinated autonomism, but it is also a case of back-to-back colonialism over 500 years. To date, the relationship with the U.S. Congress is colonial in form and substance. It is an unincorporated territory of the U.S.,[7] and it is subject to the plenary powers of the U.S. Congress under the Territory Clause of the U.S. Constitution.[8] A series of decisions by the Supreme Court, dating from the period 1901–22, known as the *Insular Cases*, created the category of "unincorporated territories." It held that the inhabitants of these areas only enjoyed the protection of those provisions of the Constitution deemed as "fundamental" by the Court, in the absence of congressional action making other provisions applicable.[9] The political status quo in Puerto Rico is known as the *Estado Libre Asociado* (ELA) (literally, "free associated state"), established in 1952.

Fourth, the extent and depth of the multidimensional crisis facing Puerto Rico are at present unparalleled in any other cases included in this special issue. Puerto Rico has been in a fiscal/economic meltdown in the last ten years, in a colonial political limbo for over 100 years, and has faced a very hostile Trump administration. Fifth, the pandemic of 2020–21 is the third natural disaster of antediluvian proportions that has hit the island in a very short time span. Hurricane María struck in September 2017 and was the greatest natural disaster in a century; earthquakes since December 2019 have destroyed urban areas in the south, and now Puerto Rico is confronted with the pandemic. Throughout these years, the response by the federal government, controlled by the Trumpist ethnonationalist Republican Party, was uniformly sluggish and half-hearted.

Sixth, the substate national movement of Puerto Rico, in its internal heterogeneity and political orientation, is different from some of the others examined in this special issue. Contrary to cases such as Scotland, Catalunya, Euskadi, or Québec, in the last 50 years, the pro-independence orientation has been quite weak, contending with a historically hegemonic autonomism while the pro-federalism orientation has grown tremendously.

Peripheral multinationalism and the United States as a multinational democracy

Because of the peculiarities of Puerto Rico as a territory of the U.S., we need to start by specifying in what sense the United States is multinational, what the national cleavage at issue is here and the national frictions or tensions it may generate. There are some forms of multinationalism that came about as a result of a long historical trajectory that brought together formerly distinct nations within the same state structure as the modern state developed in the 17th and 18th centuries. This pattern of "coming together" multinationalism is exemplified by the histories of Scotland/United Kingdom as a dynastic union and Catalonia/Spain as an incorporating union, respectively.[10] Another pattern of multinationalism is that of more recent history, whereby a culturally/linguistically/nationally distinct territory has been acquired by a much larger power, usually as a result of 19th- or 20th-century imperial expansionism. With the passage of time, that relationship tends to mature and acquires an aura of stability, although not necessarily inevitability. This "joined together" pattern of multinationalism is exemplified by the history of Puerto Rico since the late 19th century. Furthermore, because of the asymmetries in size, power, population, resources, and wealth between the island and the continental United States, at present, the multinationalism that Puerto Rico represents for the United States' federal political system is a form of "peripheral multi-nationalism." Although such multinationalism is a concrete historical reality, it does not have strong reverberations in the central state or (to date) major political consequences for the polity that manages the central state, contrary to other cases of multinationalism, such as the Catalonia-Spain relationship or the Québec-Canada relationship.

The United States has been extraordinarily diverse in its ethnic and racial composition for over two centuries. Juan Linz famously distinguished between state-nations and nation-states. Many states show cultural diversity, but for Linz the world can be divided into: (a) states that exhibit profound ethnic and national diversity; (b) states that exhibit great racial/ethnic or cultural diversity; and (c) states with a single culturally homogeneous dominant nation.[11] According to this typology, states of the first type are "robustly" multinational societies, such as Canada, Spain, Belgium, or India. In the second category, we could place Switzerland. In the third category, there are societies such as Portugal, Japan and most of the Scandinavian societies. Only by totally ignoring the presence of Puerto Rico and of Puerto Ricans in the history of the United States since the late 19th century could we see the United States as a society of the second type. I argue instead that the presence of Puerto Rico within the outer sphere of the U.S. federal political system for over a century and the presence of nearly 10 million Puerto Ricans on both the island and the mainland turns the United States into a multinational democracy, although its multinationalism is closer to the "peripheral" multinationalism model rather than Linz's more standard, "robustly" multinational sociological motif. Yet, for example, Linz sees Italy as "robustly multinational," principally by virtue of the presence of French-speaking Valle d'Aosta and German-speaking South Tyrol (and less so Friuli-Venezia-Giulia) in Italy's periphery.[12] Puerto Rico has greater demographic, political, and overall economic weight than these peripheral regions of Italy. Using Linz's own standards, therefore, Puerto Rico and Puerto Ricans turn the United States into a multinational democracy embodying a "peripheral multinationalism." Regarding national divides, furthermore, the U.S. clearly has a *Staatsvolk*: there is a dominant majority nation composed of a panoply of "white" groups whose ancestors came to the U.S. from Europe.[13]

One of the political cleavages in the U.S. at present is essentially about national identity and national divides. There are the more progressive politicians, such as Bernie Sanders and Alexandria Ocasio Cortez, who are starting to envision the U.S. as multinational or multiethnic, seeking to "'unite people who seek the advantages of membership of a common political unit, but differ markedly in descent, language, and culture,' [and who] reject the strongly integrationist or assimilationist objectives of national and/or post-national federalists, and see these as nation destroying rather than nation building."[14] This vision of the progressive wing of the Democratic Party is strongly contested by the rise of a renewed "white" ethnonational vision ensconced in the Republican party and embodied by Trumpist right wing ethnonational populism. The fate of Puerto Rico and the welfare of all Puerto Ricans hinges on the resolution of this debate within the majority nation of the United States.

U.S. national identity, multinationalism, and national divides

Faced with the growth of immigration from Latin America and the Spanish Caribbean, and the consequent growth of a Spanish-speaking minority, major political thinkers in the U.S. have reframed and reformulated their perspective on U.S. national identity. One of the most famous of these restatements is that of Samuel Huntington. He wrote that the U.S. has a core national culture that he denominates "Anglo-Protestant." The accompanying "American Creed" of political principles, including democracy, liberty, private property and rule of law, constitute this culture. He believes that until about the 1970s, the U.S. was indeed defined by race, ethnicity, ideology and culture. According to him, race and ethnicity are no longer relevant for the configuration of U.S. national identity, because people see themselves as a multiethnic, multiracial society. The "American Creed," as initially put forth by Jefferson and many others, was viewed as a defining core element of U.S. identity. However, the Creed itself is a product of the very distinct original Anglo-Protestant culture of the founding settlers 200 years ago, and essential elements of that culture include the English language, Christianity, religious piety, the English lineage of the rule of law, individual rights and the belief that it is possible to create a "city on the hill."[15] This Anglo-Protestant culture of the founding settlers has been central to U.S. national identity for over three centuries, and it is what U.S citizens have used to point to their commonalities and distinguish them as a nation distinct from other nations. Huntington stresses the continuing centrality of Anglo-Protestant culture to U.S. national identity, which is the core culture of the 17th- and 18th-century settlers who founded U.S. society. He distinguishes between culture and ancestry: one cannot change skin color or one's ancestors, but people can change or adapt their culture. Because cultural identity is fungible, the Anglo-Protestant culture is available to anyone of any race or ethnicity in the United States.

In Huntington's worldview, the core national Anglo-Protestant culture is perilously threatened by a combination of factors, but especially by the wave of immigration that began in the 1960s, bringing to the U.S. people mainly from the Americas and Asia. Most importantly, "never before in American history has close to a majority of immigrants spoken a single non-English language…" referring to Latin American immigrants, especially those coming from Mexico.[16]

Clearly, Huntington is not one to cherish the multiethnic heritage of the U.S., but even more importantly, he is hostile to notions of multinationalism and multilingualism. He rejects territorial pluralism, liberal integrationism and accommodation via multiculturalism and embraces a form of hard assimilationism in his approach to multinationalism in the United States. He prefers to envision the United States as a unitary, unilingual, mononational, centralized, symmetrical, national federation. Yet, even from his cursory treatment of Puerto Rico, he does seem to recognize that Puerto Rico is different, in light of its distinctive history. He acknowledges that there are many in the U.S. who are not immigrants nor descendants of the original English settlers: some are descendants of conquered peoples. Thus, "the distinctive character of the Indians and Puerto Ricans as in but not fully of the American republic is reflected in the arrangements negotiated with them for reservations and tribal governments, on the one hand, and commonwealth status, on the other."[17] Even Huntington acknowledges that Puerto Rico and Puerto Ricans turn the United States into a multinational democracy embodying a peripheral multinationalism. Yet, the view of the U.S. national identity that Huntington holds is inimical to Puerto Rico and to any prospect of accommodating it as a constituent unit of the federation. Huntington's understanding of U.S. national identity fails to recognize or even tolerate Puerto Rico with its distinctive societal culture, that is, a "culture which provides its members with meaningful ways of life across the full range of human activities... encompassing both public and private spheres. These cultures tend to be territorially concentrated and based on a shared language." In the United States, Puerto Rico is the paradigmatic case.[18]

Huntington's contribution to U.S. national identity is one of the most distinguished of its kind. Although it was controversial and has been criticized,[19] this Huntingtonian view of U.S. national identity is shared by many in "Trumpworld," albeit implicitly and unconsciously. In recent years, the rise of Trumpism and the transformation of the Republican Party have energized those who envision an ethnonationalist view of U.S. national identity. In fact, with the emergence of Trumpism, the most likely scenario for the future of the U.S. is the least inclusive and the least plural scenario of the ones Huntington envisioned: a political momentum seems to be building to sustain a nativist, white-majority nation reaction that would revive ancestral racial and ethnic concepts of U.S. national identity. This, of course, is the sort of national divide that is not a favorable development for the accommodation and the fair treatment of Puerto Rico within the U.S. and has multiple ramifications, including the Republican federal government's foot-dragging in its response to the COVID-19 crisis and the other natural disasters.

Trumpism, the new ethnonationalism, and Puerto Rico

As shown above, the Trumpist variant of U.S. ethnonationalism is reminiscent of the Huntingtonian thesis, but the unfavorable treatment given to Puerto Rico is motivated by political developments that have exacerbated national divides in the U.S. and which feed off and profit from national cleavages. Since its founding, U.S. political culture has been an amalgam of egalitarian liberal ideologies combined with ideological discourses that promoted cultural, linguistic, ethnic, national, racial, gender hierarchies. Unequal, ascriptive, group-differentiated categories have coexisted with liberal democratic institutions over the last two centuries. Thus, U.S. political developments are best visualized as representing the interaction of multiple political traditions, including liberalism, republicanism, and ascriptive forms of Americanism. The defining feature of U.S. political culture has not been its liberal, republican, or "ascriptive Americanist" elements, but a "more complex pattern of apparently inconsistent combinations of the traditions, accompanied by recurring conflicts."[20] The acquisition of Puerto Rico (and other U.S. colonies) in the late 19th century illustrates the multiple traditions in U.S. political culture. It was acquired as a colony as part of the U.S. elite's *mission civilisatrice* and the "White Man's Burden." The "varied assortment of inferior races" inhabiting those territories "could not be allowed to vote." Eventually, U.S. citizenship was imposed on Puerto Rico's residents, but as second-class citizens, and they were eventually designated as inhabitants of a liminal status: an "unincorporated territory."[21] This new civic status was invented principally for Puerto Ricans, and it embodied the tension between liberalism's egalitarian promise and inegalitarian ideologies that disdained ethnicities, nations and races that were deemed "inferior" by the majority nation of the United States. These "ascriptive forms of Americanism" have at certain points in history shaped perceptions of United States national identity and fed state nationalism in the U.S. These perceptions are critical because they delineate the contours of the national divide and the sorts of ethnonational tensions that can have an impact on Puerto Rico and Puerto Ricans.

Modernity developed within the boundaries of the nation-state and "equal treatment before the law became a privilege reserved for nationals."[22] In modern times, nationalist thinking has led to a territorialization of the social imagination: "the territory occupied by the national community at the same time traces the ideal frontiers of the polity...."[23] In modernity, equals must be governed by likes, but the U.S. citizens of Puerto Rico are not perceived as equals nor alike and are still seen by the mainstream in the continental USA as "foreign in a domestic sense," even after 123 years. Nowhere has this been more evident than in the way Trumpism has treated Puerto Rico during the pandemic crisis and the other epochal natural disasters the island has endured since 2017. To understand how Trumpism-in-power actually operates, we need to account for the transformation of the Republican party.

The adoption of Trumpist ethnonationalism by the Republican Party is the story of how the party has resolved the "conservative dilemma" that other center-right parties (such as the British Conservative Party) in the late 19th century and 20th century had to resolve. Center-right parties have faced an electoral disadvantage since they emerged as representatives of small elites and programmatically unwilling to adopt social spending programs. To compensate for their theoretically small social base, conservative parties have sought to succeed electorally by shifting to the middle and relying on nationalism, identity politics, racism, primeval emotionalism and in general stoking social resentments and amassing electoral support by appealing to those sectors of the population that are susceptible to such appeals.[24] While they have become increasingly reliant on white working-class voters, Republicans segregate their plutocratic economic strategies from their electoral stratagems, relying increasingly on radicalizing voters and getting them to see electoral politics as "us versus them" identity wars. As Hacker and Pierson argue, they use racial appeals, disparage government generally and Democrats specifically, and invoke a primeval national identity around whiteness, conservative Christianity, the rural-urban divide, gun ownership, reifying the English language and adopting an ethnic nationalism, all the while maintaining the party's plutocratic habitus aiming to benefit the richest strata.[25]

In sum, the Republican Party has deepened racial, cultural, and national divides in the United States, and the obsequious submissiveness of Republican politicians vis-à-vis Donald Trump can only be explained by recognizing the extent to which Trump has used the discourse of outrage to unify the dwindling but intense white ethnonationalist voting block that placed him on the presidential pedestal.[26] A recent study by the V-Dem Institute at the University of Gothenburg, Sweden, has shown that the Republican Party has shifted in an illiberal direction and is currently closer in its rhetoric to authoritarian parties such as the AKP in Turkey and Fidesz in Hungary.[27] A new white identity politics has been in crescendo, and Trumpism has ridden the crest of this reinvigorated white identity. Whiteness in the U.S. is everywhere, but it is sometimes said to be invisible. "The unmasked category against which difference is constructed, whiteness never has to speak its name, never has to acknowledge its role as an organizing principle in social and cultural relations."[28] By the 1990s, European immigrants (including Italians, Irish, Polish, etc.) had assimilated to mainstream culture, narrowly defined in the 19th century as Anglo-Protestant. However, white identity nowadays has content, and today we can see that "whites who identify with their racial group share a set of common ideas about their group and attach meaning to their race."[29]

One of the important components of white identity today is its association with a particularistic vision of U.S. national identity. At its very founding, the U.S. was defined as a nation with a culture and traditions inherited from its Anglo-Saxon Protestant fore-mothers. Whiteness in the U.S. is often viewed as synonymous with being "American," and the majority nation identity of the U.S. is, in turn, defined by whiteness. "Today, this association is so tightly bound that it pervades whites' subconscious.... Americans automatically and unconsciously associate 'American' with 'white.' The greater the extent to which whites demonstrated this 'American = White' association, the stronger their reported national identity was. Most white Americans see themselves as archetypal members of the nation."[30] The empirical findings by Jardina show that "whites high on racial identity are clustered at the high end of the American identity scale.... Close to 69 percent of whites high on racial identity indicated that their American identity is extremely important to them."[31] These associations between white racial identity and national identity have important corollaries. Strong national identifiers are more likely to establish hard boundaries around their imagined national group, and these are likely to be more exclusive, crafting a non-pluralistic normative idea of who represents a "true" American. Empirically, do whites in the U.S. with strong identities adopt more exclusive, hard boundaries around their conceptualization of U.S. national identity, fore-grounding their white, Christian, English-speaking heritage?[32] Yes, "whites with higher levels of racial identity are more supportive of exclusionary boundaries ... [and] white racial identity is an important component of adopting particular beliefs about who is a "true" American and who is not."[33] Thus, white racial identity is coupled with a par-ticular vision of U.S. national identity. Whites with a strong racial identity are much more likely to believe in exclusionary definitions of what it means to be an "American" and to insist that, in order to be a genuine "American," such traits as the use of the English language are indispensable. "Their understanding of race and national identity is very much an affirmation of the dominant group's ability to capture and define the identity of the country."[34] Trumpism has promoted the hardening of this new white racial identity, which promotes a vision of U.S. national identity that is unsympathetic to multinationalism and thus inimical to Puerto Rico.

Trumpism, the new ethnonationalism, and the federal response to crises in Puerto Rico

Donald Trump has been very explicit and very direct in letting the world know how much he disdains Puerto Rico and Puerto Ricans. This pattern of denigration is evi-denced by Trump's handling of Hurricane María and has continued to date during the pandemic. A few days after the devastation of Hurricane María, Trump suggested that people on the island were ingrates responsible for much of their suffering, setting a new low that was "even meaner than his usual harangues and self-aggrandizement." It called into question whether Mr. Trump grasps and accepts the responsibilities of his office when he imperiously suggested that federal emergency aid and workers could not be maintained on the island "forever...." The contrast between how he regarded hurricane victims in Texas and Florida and those in Puerto Rico was evident: "Trump prefers to belittle Puerto Rico and question its entitlement to recovery help."[35] In contrast to the approach he took with Florida and Texas, Trump assailed the very people he was supposed to be assisting. On his visit to San Juan a few weeks after the near category 5 hurricane, he amused himself by throwing paper towels at an astonished and shell-shocked crowd, and he mocked the island, stating at a news conference during that visit that "I hate to tell you, Puerto Rico, you've thrown our budget a little out of whack, because we've spent a lot of money on Puerto Rico." As the then-governor stated: "We are not asking for better treatment or less treatment... We are asking for equal treatment....not asking for anything that another U.S. jurisdiction... wouldn't be asking at this juncture."[36]

The former chief of the Department of Homeland Security, Miles Taylor, recently confirmed that Trump, adding insult to injury, during the aftermath of Hurricane María, once asked whether the U.S. could swap Puerto Rico for resource-rich Greenland "and frequently made disparaging remarks about the Puerto Rican people." For Trump, Puerto Rico "was dirty and the people were poor." Furthermore, "when asked if he thought Trump was making a joke, Taylor insisted that on multiple occasions, the President had "expressed deep animus toward the Puerto Rican people behind the scenes."[37] Trump's public policy toward Puerto Rico can be described "as lack of respect for human life, inaction in the face of tragedy and, often, racism and open discrimination against the people of Puerto Rico."[38] Since 2017, what we have seen is a differentiated treatment for Puerto Rico. As one former Resident Commissioner of Puerto Rico in Congress stated: "We do not receive equal treatment, and we should, because we are U.S citizens. There should not be two different U.S. citizenships. One should be treated as a U.S. citizen wherever one lives. That's what's wrong with present status of Puerto Rico: the way the federal government treats us."[39] Even the current Resident Commissioner, a staunch Trumpist, repudiated Trump's open disrespect toward Puerto Rico and Puerto Ricans.[40] As Congressman Darren Soto affirmed, in the last three years, only half of the federal funds promised to Puerto Rico for its reconstruction had been disbursed.[41]

Trumpism and the federal response to the COVID-19 pandemic in relation to Puerto Rico and Puerto Ricans

Regarding the impact on Puerto Rico, a number of factors have combined to aggravate the pandemic's impact on the island: the general hostility of the U.S. federal administration, the fragility of the Puerto Rico government given its long-running fiscal/economic debacle, the lack of legitimacy of the unelected governor of Puerto Rico during 2019–20, and the poor conditions of the public health system and infrastructure, given that it is still reeling from Hurricanes María and Irma. With 105,020 confirmed COVID-19 cases, 105,399 probable cases, and 2,182 deaths as of 14 April 2021, the island has been hit particularly hard by the pandemic.[42] Given its status as a part of the U.S. federal political system and the open border between the island and the U.S. 50 states (and the ease of travel), many of Puerto Rico's challenges are a function of what is occurring on the continent and the U.S. federal government's response. "Puerto Rico was still reeling from the structural and economic damage caused by hurricanes María and Irma, and by a sequence of earthquakes in early 2020, when the coronavirus was declared a global pandemic."[43] Hence, Puerto Rico has been hit by the economic impact of the virus, in part as a result of the mismanagement of the pandemic by the Trump administration and the economic repercussions of such mismanagement. "Between February and April of 2020, nonfarm payroll employment declined by 13.5% in Puerto Rico.... With 43.1% of the population living in poverty... few of the island's residents are positioned to weather the economic crisis without assistance from the U.S. government."[44]

The pandemic has hit Puerto Rico's elderly population especially hard and is compounded by the deterioration in federal support for elderly care, in large part because of the way Puerto Rico has been treated by the Trump administration. Many elderly people on the island depend on Medicare for their healthcare, just as on the U.S. mainland. However, "spending per Puerto Rican enrollee is lower than that of any U.S. state" even though island residents pay the same payroll taxes as anyone else. "Also, recent funding cuts in Medicare have caused severe financial losses to the Puerto Rican healthcare system...."[45] Furthermore, "federal grants awarded to Puerto Rico's Medicare system through the Affordable Care Act (ACA) expired in 2017 and were not renewed by the federal government post-Hurricane María. Federal financial shortfalls and austerity measures have become a central feature defining the Puerto Rican healthcare system and have increased barriers to health care access and high-quality health care among Puerto Rico's older adult population. These health care challenges are further exacerbated by delayed and low Medicare reimbursement payments...."[46]

The pattern of the Trump administration vis-à-vis Puerto Rico is clear in the last three years: "since 2017, Puerto Rico has faced unprecedented devastation from hurricanes, earthquakes, COVID-19, and long-standing fiscal and economic crises that demand aggressive federal action in response."[47] Instead, the Trump administration set out "to deliberately marginalize and harm Puerto Rico and prevent the island from having any chance of rebuilding its economy or infrastructure."[48] In addition to all the aforementioned actions, in February 2020, President Trump threatened to veto $4.7 billion in emergency aid package intended to help Puerto Rico recover from a series of damaging earthquakes, and the Trump administration imposed severe restrictions on billions of dollars in emergency relief to Puerto Rico.[49]

Regarding the impact on Puerto Ricans who have moved to the continent, the nation is both on the island and on the continent, but the combined effects of the fiscal/economic stagnation and the successive natural disasters have heightened out-migration from the island. According to the 2019 U.S. Census Bureau's Population Estimates, the island's population declined from 3.7 million in 2010 to 3.1 million in 2019. "Taken together, the post-Hurricane María exodus represents one of the most significant movements of Puerto Ricans to the U.S. mainland in the island's history in terms of both volume and duration."[50] Puerto Ricans on the mainland now number close to 6 million. The explanandum for the population shift from the island to the continent "stems from an unequal relationship—a colonial relationship between the U.S. and Puerto Rico—that has resulted in dire economic conditions on the island such as: deindustrialization; high government debt; high unemployment; corruption in the financial sector … and the strangling of the Puerto Rican economy by the Jones Act."[51] In the U.S federation, the COVID-19 death rates for each age group "are significantly higher for the Latinx population than for the white population. In fact, among those aged 35–44, Latinx Americans are nearly nine times as likely to die from COVID-19 as white Americans. These findings are troubling, but they are consistent with other analysis of the CDC data."[52]

As the CDC puts it in its report on COVID-19 and the Health Equity Considerations and Racial and Ethnic Minority Groups, "there is increasing evidence that some racial and ethnic minority groups are being disproportionately affected by Covid-19." Some of the factors explaining this include inequities in the social determinants of health and discrimination.[53] The Trump administration's mismanagement of the pandemic has led to a disastrous impact on Latinos in the federation, including Puerto Ricans in major cities such as New York or Chicago. Trump's bungled response includes the failure to provide necessary personal protective equipment for frontline workers, failure to guarantee social distancing measures everywhere, failure to adhere to the values of the Enlightenment of truth and science, failure to develop a federal contact tracing program, failure to be truthful about what medicines could really help to ameliorate the lethality of the virus, failure to provide a centralized and coherent response and failure to implement the simplest and most necessary public health measure: mandating that everyone needs to wear a mask. Thus, "the country's response to the pandemic remains hampered by medical supply shortages. As masks, gloves and other protective equipment become more available, it is clear that all essential workers require them, not just emergency and medical personnel. That includes janitors, home health aides, delivery people, grocery and farm workers and sanitation workers …. In New York City, as in many cities, much of the municipal work force is black or Hispanic."[54] In New York City in April 2020, the preliminary death rate for Hispanic people was about 22 persons per 100,000, whereas it was 10 persons per 100,000 for majority nation whites.[55] Federal data reveal that "Black and Latino people have been disproportionately affected by the coronavirus in a widespread manner that spans the country, throughout hundreds of counties in urban, suburban and rural areas, and across all age groups."[56] According to a report by the *New York Times*, "for the 206 counties with at least 5,000 Latino residents analyzed by *The Times*, 178 have higher infection rates for Latino residents than for white residents."[57] The pandemic has also significantly harmed the economic situation of U.S. Hispanics. By April 2020, the unemployment rate among Hispanics had risen to 18.5% from 4.8% in February.[58] Even Joe Biden, who underperformed with "Latinos" in 2020, actively campaigned in Florida as the November 3 election date approached, trying to reach out to Puerto Ricans there and emphasizing the reality that "Latinos were contracting and dying from the coronavirus and suffering economically at disproportionately high rates, and that president Trump had mishandled the pandemic."[59]

Trumpism and the federal response to the Hurricane María disaster
Three years before the global pandemic began in 2020, Puerto Rico had already been clobbered by another once-in-a-century natural disaster: the double impact of

Hurricanes María and Irma in September 2017. The federal government of the Trump era was sluggish and negligent in its response to this disaster, and Puerto Rico was given differential treatment vis-à-vis other parts of the United States also impacted by major hurricanes. Several studies have compared the federal response to hurricane disaster in Texas and Florida with Puerto Rico. The analysis shows that the federal response was faster, better, and more generous with respect to money and staffing to Hurricanes Harvey and Irma in 2017 in Florida and Texas. In that same hurricane season of 2017, Puerto Rico experienced a direct hit from an even more powerful storm, Hurricane María. "Assuming that disaster responses should be commensurate to the degree of storm severity and need of the population, the federal response is questionable and the degree of variation between the disaster responses is problematic."[60] In terms of FEMA dollars awarded to individuals and families, within the first 9 days after Harvey and Irma hit, their survivors had received nearly $100 million awarded to individuals and families, whereas María survivors had only received slightly over $6 million in recovery assistance. Federal staffing is critical to recovery efforts: within 9 days of landfall, there were 30,000 federal employees posted in Texas, 16,200 posted in Florida and 10,000 posted in Puerto Rico. At the peak, there were 19,000 posted in Puerto Rico and 31,000 in Texas, even though Puerto Rico suffered complete destruction of its electric grid and communications infrastructure and greater devastation to its housing stock. Differential treatment is also observable based on the delivery and timing of federally appropriated funds to the impacted communities. Congress responded to these disasters with three separate spending bills between September and December 2017. In September 2017, Congress authorized $15.25 billion in Hurricanes Harvey and Irma disaster relief. A second bill was passed a month later, which provided $18.67 billion for the Disaster Relief Fund for all three hurricanes. In this second bill, up to $4.9 billion was allocated to Puerto Rico in the "form of a Community Disaster Loan, as opposed to the CDB *grants* allocated in September to Texas and Florida. On 9 January, Puerto Rico was denied that $4.9 billion loan from the October bill…with the Treasury Department seeking further proof of lack of liquidity."[61] Putting aside issues of infrastructure fragility and geography, "issues of racial bias and perceptions of differential citizenship all may have affected the appropriation and delivery of resources and funding to affected areas in each hurricane."[62]

A report by the UN High Commissioner on Human Rights concluded that Puerto Rico in 2017, one month after María, remained without an effective federal response. Hurricanes are natural, but disasters are political. "In the case of the federal government, there was an obvious unequal treatment in comparison with U.S. states, related to the condition as 'second-class' colonial citizens. The OHCHR observed 'the dissimilar urgency and priority given to the emergency response in Puerto Rico, compared to the U.S. states affected by hurricanes in recent months.' For instance, FEMA has only deployed 1700 personnel to Puerto Rico and the Virgin Islands since María, whereas it sent 2600 personnel to the Gulf Coast after Harvey."[63] President Trump's visit after Hurricane María showed a kind of imperial disdain: "only 3 weeks after the hurricane, he complained that we were 'throwing the U.S. budget out of whack,' tweeted that he could not keep FEMA and other federal officials in Puerto Rico 'forever,' and they were ungrateful and wanted 'everything done by us.'"[64] As the report on "FEMA

Mismanaged the Commodity Distribution Process in Response to Hurricanes Irma and María" by the Office of Inspector General of Homeland Security stated: "FEMA lost visibility of about 38 percent of its commodity shipments to Puerto Rico, worth an estimated $257 million. Commodities delivered to Puerto Rico took an average of 69 days to reach their final destination. Inadequate FEMA contractor oversight contributed to the lost visibility and delayed commodity shipments."[65] In early 2020, the Trump administration imposed severe limitations on billions of dollars in emergency relief for Puerto Rico, including blocking spending on the island's electrical infrastructure. Representative Nydia Velázquez (D-NY) called these restrictions disdainful and contemptuous: "'Why is Puerto Rico always subjected to different standards when it comes to this administration?'"[66]

Crises and their impact on Puerto Rico's national movement

The COVID-19 pandemic, together with the recent major hurricanes and multiple earthquakes, plus the economic/fiscal crisis, has shaken Puerto Rico's politics. The years 2019–21 have brought historic changes to the national movement and the political party system of Puerto Rico.

Puerto Rico's national movement shows a familiar pattern, typical of contemporary stateless nations. For much of the 20th century and to date, the national movement has been transitioning between what Miroslav Hroch labeled Phase B and Phase C, in his periodization of national movements.[67] That is, it has attained the phase where the national movement is "massified," fully recognizing and asserting its status as a substate national (or distinct) society. It is also internally heterogenous and exhibits three basic political orientations: within the national movement, there has been a component of the movement that has always favored independence and another component that has sought to accommodate the sub-state nation within the U.S. federal system with different formulas for autonomism.[68]

A third component is internally diverse, and a portion of it (at times quite minoritarian) recognizes Puerto Rico as a distinct society and opts for federalism and federation as its preferred formula for accommodating Puerto Rico within the U.S. federation as the 51st state. Another portion of this third component seems to be majoritarian and explicitly sees Puerto Rico only as an ethnic minority and sees the U.S. as its nation.

Puerto Rico's independentist and autonomist parties are thus clearly sub-state national political parties because they affirm and defend Puerto Rico as a nation or at least a distinct society, while the actually-existing federalist party is either a borderline sub-state national party or a majority-nation national party.[69] All three of Puerto Rico's major political parties have been in existence for over half a century and all three belong to the regional and ethnic parties *familles spirituelles* as conceptualized by Klaus von Beyme and his nine major "party groups that can be considered under the same name."[70] The sub-state regional party family includes well-known parties such as the Scottish National Party, the Südtiroler Volkspartei and the Partido Nacionalista Vasco.[71] Sub-state regional parties have their electoral base solely within the sub-state region, and may be willing at times to trade off influence over the center for more (perceived) autonomy. They may also identify with a linguistic/ethnic/national sub-state identity, and in their ideology may prioritize the constitutional relationship with the central state, over the political economy or state-society axes.[72]

The three major parties in Puerto Rico are the autonomist *Partido Popular Democrático* (PPD), the federalist *Partido Nuevo Progresista* (PNP), and the independentist *Partido Independentista Puertorriqueño* (PIP). Puerto Rico has a variant of a two-and-a-half party system in which only the PPD and PNP have been in power,[73] and the PIP has been a testimonial, moral presence that people generally respect because of its advocacy of self-determination and independence. However, the PIP has not been able to elect any of its candidates for governor, does not have a major presence in any of the two chambers of the legislative assembly, and has not succeeded in capturing major municipalities. Nevertheless, the PIP is heard, respected, and plays a role in the party system. If we look at the historical pattern between 1952 and 1968, during the early part of this period, the PPD generally had greater strength than the PNP and was the dominant party. However, since 1968, the parties have exchanged their positions, and the PNP in recent times has had greater electoral success than the PPD.

The 3 November 2020 election, however, represents a change in the historical orientation of Puerto Rico's party system and may lead to an electoral realignment and the establishment of a more plural, multi-party system. For the first time in many decades, several important new developments occurred.

First, a new political party successfully emerged and ran credible candidates all over the island. The *Movimiento Victoria Ciudadana* (MVC) is a center-left party that de-emphasized the center-periphery axis while foregrounding the need to reconstruct and cleanse Puerto Rico's government and put an end to clientelism, Trumpist abuse and disdain, corruption and bad governance. MVC was led by two young, hip, and attractive figures: Alexandra Lúgaro and Manuel Natal. The MVC candidate for governor (Lúgaro) received 14.21% of the vote, coming in third, behind the winning PNP candidate, who received 32.93%, and the second-place PPD candidate, who received 31.56%.[74] The MVC was also successful in getting two senators and two representatives elected for the Legislative Assembly. The MVC candidate for mayor of San Juan (Natal) almost won the mayoralty, but in the end came short by a few votes.

It should be noted as well that another political party was also successful in establishing itself in 2020. *Proyecto Dignidad* (PD) is a right-wing party that brought into the public arena the ideological mantra of right wing (allegedly "religious") fundamentalists, reminiscent of some of the ideological stances of Vox in Spain, or Steve Bannon. The candidate for governor of this party received 6.9% of the vote.

Second, for the first time in decades, the third major party (the PIP) performed much better electorally, led by the charismatic Juan Dalmau, who emphasized social justice and good government and resisted Trumpist federal overreach and mistreatment while deemphasizing the center-periphery axis. Dalmau was the candidate for governor and received a historic high (for the PIP) of 13.72% of the vote. The PIP got one senator and one representative elected in the Legislative Assembly.

Third, the pro-statehood and federalist PNP candidates for governor (Pierluisi) and resident commissioner were victorious, and there was also a plebiscite question posed to the electorate that resulted in a historic milestone: in a Statehood Yes or No question, the Yes option received 52.3% of the vote and the No received 47.6%. For the first time ever, the statehood option has received plurality support. When combined with the earlier 2012 plebiscite in which 54% of the voters declared that the present constitutional status (*Estado Libre Asociado*) was unacceptable, the citizens of Puerto Rico have now voted in such a way that the current colonial status quo is illegitimate and disliked by a clear majority, while another non-ambiguous plurality has expressed its support for becoming the 51st constituent unit of the U.S. federation.

Therefore, the 3 November 2020 election highlights an important evolution in Puerto Rico's political party system: a challenge has been mounted against the two-and-a-half party system, and we may be seeing the birth of a more plural party system with more players. In addition, I would highlight the successful irruption of a new party (MVC) that is left of center and challenges the colonial status quo, without being expressly in favor of either statehood or independence. Importantly, the 52% support for federalism and statehood in the plebiscite is an important historical marker and will be the fulcrum for pressuring the Biden-Harris administration to act, and respect Puerto Rico's self-determination preferences.

In the summer of 2019, mass protests erupted over a scandalous telegram chat involving then PNP governor, Ricardo Rosselló, and eventually that governor had to resign. For the first in history a sitting governor had to resign. Next in the line of constitutional succession was attorney Wanda Vázquez and she substituted the disgraced governor. That novel political event, combined with the calamity of Hurricane María, plus the long-running fiscal/economic crisis, and further combined with the present COVID-19 global pandemic, ignited the perfect political storm in 2020. The electoral events of November 2020, as we have discussed above, was the culmination of these major crises' impacts on Puerto Rican society.

Conclusion

The wider federal political system we call the United States is a multinational democracy: the existence of Puerto Rico in the periphery of the U.S. state apparatus is a de facto form of peripheral multinationalism and a meaningful national divide. Yet, Puerto Rico is in six significant ways different from some of the other cases of stateless nationhood in this special issue. It is also different given that no other case in this special issue has faced a central state with a federal government that, during the COVID-19 crisis (and the other natural disasters), has shown such a degree of callousness and disdain in its response to these calamitous events. Trumpism's intolerant vision of U.S. national identity and its reconstitution of a form of ethnonational and exclusionary form of "Americanism" is the driving force behind the negative animus toward Puerto Rico and Puerto Ricans. The COVID-19 crisis, plus the cumulative effects of the previous crises, has had a significant effect on Puerto Rico's sub-state national movement and its political party system.

People of many political persuasions find Puerto Rico's current political arrangement inadequate. In the 2012 referendum, 54% of the population rejected the status quo. As U.S. Senator Ron Wyden declared: "the current relationship undermines the United States' moral standing in the world. For a nation founded on the principles of democracy and the consent of the governed, how much longer can America allow a condition to persist in which nearly four million U.S. citizens do not have a vote in the government that makes the national laws which affect their daily lives?"[75] Regarding political, social and economic rights (including fiscal rights and privileges), the second-class U.S. citizenship of Puerto Ricans exhibits a remarkable degree of differentiation vis-à-vis the first class U.S. citizenship that is enjoyed in the federation due to its status as an unincorporated territory. The inadequate and discriminatory federal response under the Trump administration to the COVID-19 crisis and the other natural disasters is principally attributable to Trumpism's negative disposition toward Puerto Rico and Puerto Ricans, above and beyond the fact that the residents of Puerto Rico have a second-class U.S. citizenship. It is also evident that the Trump administration was in general incompetent and willfully negligent in managing the COVID-19 crisis in all of the U.S. Again, with respect to Puerto Rico and Puerto Ricans, it was especially disdainful and callous, aggravating the situation in Puerto Rico. In addition, when a federal administration in the U.S. acts incompetently, it is usually the most vulnerable and the most marginalized minority populations that suffer the most, and this dynamic also helps to understand Trump's mistreatment of Puerto Rico and Puerto Ricans.

Trump left office on 20 January 2021, but Trumpism remains a powerful political force. At the time of this writing, there are two bills before Congress addressing the resolution of Puerto Rico's status: one calls for a binding process of consultation through the establishment of a constitutional convention, and the other seeks to implement the referendum result of 3 November 2020 and set Puerto Rico on the path to becoming the 51st state.[76] The next few years will be critical for the future of Puerto Rico.

Notes

1. Ronald Watts, *Comparing Federal Systems*, 2nd ed. (Montréal: McGill-Queens University Press, 1999).
2. Alain Gagnon and James Tully, eds., *Multinational Democracies* (Cambridge: Cambridge University Press, 2001), 2.
3. Michael Keating, *Plurinational Democracy* (Oxford: Oxford University Press, 2001), 27.
4. Nancy Morris, *Puerto Rico: Culture, Politics, and Identity* (Westport: Praeger, 1995).
5. Jorge Duany, *The Puerto Rican Nation on the Move: Identities on the Island and in the United States* (Chapel Hill: University of North Carolina Press, 2002).
6. Jaime Lluch, "Unpacking Political Identity: Race, Ethnicity, and Nationhood in a Federal Political System," *Ethnopolitics* 18, no. 2 (October 2018): 1–23.
7. Efrén Rivera Ramos, *The Legal Construction of Identity* (Washington, DC: APA Press, 2001).
8. T. Alexander Aleinikoff, *Semblances of Sovereignty* (Cambridge: Harvard University Press, 2002), 76).
9. Balzac v. Porto Rico, 258 U.S. 298, 312–13 (1922).
10. John H. Elliott, *Scots and Catalans: Union and Disunion* (New Haven: Yale University Press, 2018). Although these terms reminds us of Alfred Stepan's famous distinction between the origins of "coming together" versus "holding together" federations, my concepts and my intent here are completely distinguishable. Alfred Stepan, *Arguing Comparative Politics* (Oxford: Oxford University Press, 2001), 320.
11. Juan Linz, Alfred Stepan, and Yogendra Yadav, *Crafting State-Nations: India and Other Multinational Democracies* (Baltimore: Johns Hopkins University Press, 2011), 1.
12. Ibid., 228.

13. Brendan O'Leary and John McGarry, "Federation and Managing Nations," in *Multinational Federations*, edited by Michael Burgess and John Pinder (London: Routledge, 2007), 198.
14. Ibid., 188.
15. Samuel Huntington, *Who Are We: The Challenges to America's National Identity* (New York: Simon and Schuster, 2004), xvi.
16. Ibid., 19.
17. Ibid., 46.
18. Will Kymlicka, *Multicultural Citizenship* (Oxford: Oxford University Press, 1995), 76.
19. See, for example, Jack Citr, Amy Lerman, Michael Murakami, and Kathryn Pearsonal, "Testing Huntington: Is Hispanic Immigration a Threat to American Identity?," *Perspectives on Politics* 1, no. 5 (March 2007): 31–48. This article does not question the American Creed as presented in mainstream U.S. political science as much as it says that Mexican Americans do not pose the kind of national identity threat as suggested by Huntington. Instead, Citrin and his co-authors argue that available evidence is that Mexican Americans become English dominant in the second generation and that Mexican Americans do not really identify closely with any pan ethnic identity as "Latino" or "Hispanic."
20. Rogers M. Smith, "Beyond de Tocqueville, Myrdal, and Hartz: The Multiple Traditions in America," *American Political Science Review* 87 (3) 1993, 548–63, 558.
21. Ibid., 560.
22. Andreas Wimmer, *Nationalist Exclusion and Ethnic* Conflict (Cambridge: Cambridge University Press, 2002), 58.
23. Ibid., 54.
24. Jacob Hacker and Paul Pierson, *Let Them Eat Tweets: How the Right Rules in an Age of Extreme Inequality* (New York: Liveright, 2020).
25. Ibid.
26. Ibid.
27. V-Dem Institute, *New Global Data on Political Parties: V-Party*, Briefing Paper, No. 9 (26), October 2020.
28. Ashley Jardina, *White Identity Politics* (Cambridge: Cambridge University Press, 2019), 118.
29. Ibid., 119.
30. Ibid., 120.
31. Ibid., 122.
32. Ibid., 123.
33. Ibid., 126.
34. Ibid., 152.
35. "A Disaster in the White House for Puerto Rico," *New York Times Editorial*, 12 October 2017.
36. Peter Baker, "Trump Warns Storm-Ravaged Puerto Rico That Aid Won't Last Forever," *New York Times*, 12 October 2017.
37. Jeremy Blum, "Former DHS Chief: Trump Wanted to Swap Puerto Rico for Greenland," *Huffington Post*, 19 August 2020.
38. "Exjefe de Gabinete de Seguridad Interna: Trump ha tenido 'profunda animosidad' hacia el pueblo de Puerto Rico," *El Nuevo Día*, 20 August 2020.
39. "Pedro Pierluisi aseguró que Donald Trump le faltó el respeto a Puerto Rico," *El Nuevo Día*, 21 August 2020.
40. Ibid.
41. Ibid.
42. Departamento de Salud de PR, "Informe de Casos Covid-19," 14 de abril del 2021.
43. Economic Policy Institute, "Latinx Workers – Particularly Women – Face Devastating Job Losses in the Covid-19 Recession," Report, Washington, DC, 20 August 2020, 13.
44. Ibid.
45. Catherine García, Fernando I. Rivera, Marc A. Garcia, Giovani Burgos, and María P. Aranda, "Contextualizing the Covid-19 Era in Puerto Rico: Compounding Disasters and

Paralles Pandemics," *The Gerontologist,* published by Oxford UP for The Gerontological Society of America (accessed 29 October 2020).

46. Ibid.
47. Center for American Progress Action Fund, "The Trump Administration's Top 20 Actions that Have Kept Puerto Ricans in Crisis," 15 June 2020.
48. Ibid.
49. Ibid.
50. Center for Puerto Rican Studies, Hunter College, "Enduring Disasters: Puerto Rico, Three Years after Hurricane María," September, 2020, 5.
51. Catherine García et al., "Contextualizing the Covid-19 Era in Puerto Rico."
52. Economic Policy Institute.
53. CDC, Coronavirus Disease 2019, "Health Equity Considerations and Racial and Ethnic Minority Groups," 24 July 2020.
54. "How to Save Black and Hispanic Lives in a Pandemic," *New York Times,* 11 April 2020.
55. "Virus is Twice as Deadly for Black and Latino People than Whites in NYC," *New York Times,* 8 April 2020.
56. "The Fullest Look Yet at the Racial Inequity of the Coronavirus," *New York Times,* 5 July 2020.
57. Ibid.
58. Pew Research Center, "Coronavirus Economic Downturn Has Hit Latinos Especially Hard," August 2020.
59. "How Democrats Missed Trump's Appeal to Latino Voters," *New York Times,* 9 November 2020.
60. Charley Willison, Phillip M. Singer, Melissa S. Creary, and Scott L. Greer, "Quantifying Inequities in US Federal Response to Hurricane Disaster in Texas and Florida Compared with Puerto Rico," *BMJ Global Health* 4 (2019): e001191.
61. Ibid.
62. Ibid.
63. Gustavo García López, "The Multiple Layers of Environmental Injustice in Contexts of (Un)natural Disasters: The Case of Puerto Rico post-Hurricane María," *Environmental Justice* 11, no. 3 (2018): 45.
64. Ibid.
65. U.S. Department of Homeland Security, Office of Inspector General, "FEMA Mismanaged the Commodity Distribution Process in Response to Hurricanes Irma and María," 25 September 2020, OIG-20-76.
66. "Trump Attaches Severe Restrictions to Puerto Rico's Long-Delayed Disaster Aid," *New York Times,* 15 January 2020.
67. Miroslav Hroch, *Social Preconditions of National Revival in Europe: A Comparative Analysis of the Social Composition of Patriotic Groups Among the Smaller European Nations* (New York: Columbia University Press, 2000).
68. Jaime Lluch, *Visions of Sovereignty: Nationalism and Accommodation in Multinational Democracies* (Philadelphia: University of Pennsylvania Press, 2014).
69. Ibid.
70. Klaus von Beyme, *Political Parties in Western Democracies* (Aldershot: Gower, 1985), 3.
71. Lieven de Winter and Huri Türsan, eds., *Regionalist Parties in Western Europe* (London: Routledge, 1998), 204.
72. Eve Hepburn, *Using Europe: Territorial Party Strategies in a Multi-Level System* (Manchester: Manchester University Press, 2010), 48; Emanuele Massetti and Arjan Schakel, "From Class to Region: How Regionalist Parties Link (and Subsume) Left-Right into Centre-Periphery," *Party Politics* 21, no. 6 (2015): 866–86; Anwen Elias and Filippo Tronconi, "From Protest to Power: Autonomist Parties in Government," *Party Politics* 17, no. 4 (2011): 505–24.
73. Giovanni Sartori, *Parties and Party Systems: A Framework for Analysis* (Colchester: ECPR Press, 2005).

74. Comisión Estatal de Elecciones de Puerto Rico, 2020.
75. Statement of Senator Ron Wyden, Energy and Natural Resources Committee SD-366, U.S. Senate, 1 August 2013.
76. José Delgado, "Abre el Debate Formal," *El Nuevo Día*, 14 April 2021, 10.

Conclusion Looking Forward: Multinationalism and Responses to Covid-19

Stephanie Kerr

With deaths from Covid-19 at over 6.4 million by the summer of 2022, and the International Monetary Fund suggesting in January 2022 that the cost of the pandemic could hit 12.5 trillion through 2024, not to mention the extensive social and political disruption caused by both the virus and the response to it, it is safe to say that Covid-19 can be considered an exogenous shock on any given state. Throughout this volume, the authors have outlined key dynamics of the interaction between such a shock and multinationalism as an institutional arrangement, sociological fact, and political culture.

A crisis can be defined as a "sudden, negative and temporally constrained change within a system which threatens to bring about a large and unforeseen transformation of a number of identifying characteristics of that system and which urgently calls for new approaches and solutions" (Aguirresarobe, 2022, p.17). That is not to say that any crisis will be successfully met with such new approaches, but there is a perceived need or opportunity for change. Nor does the presence of a crisis erase preexisting challenges when it rears its head. The Covid-19 pandemic served to compound preexisting crises, including those that may have existed in democratic governance or quality. For instance, given the response of closing borders and intense debates over reopening and the movement of people, questions of migration have arguably become all the more politicized. This in a context where even prior to the pandemic nationalism and populism were arguably already on the rise (Boucher et al. 2021).

Using a framework of six interrelated points of interrogation, the authors have begun to flesh out how multinationalism has impacted and been impacted by the pandemic and the responses to the virus.

There are those who argued that the transnational nature of the global pandemic and its utter disregard for state borders represented a serious challenge to the very idea of nationalism, and that such a globalized problem would require a globalized solution thus undermining the role of the nation-state as both a site of governance and principal site of collective identity, others are less convinced (Woods et al. 2020). While there have certainly been attempts at collective responses, such as the vaccine sharing COVAX program, nationalism remains the dominant perspective despite the pandemic with core elements of the nationalist worldview – the particular borders and values of its own national community, arguably strengthened (Aguirresarobe 2022). Moreover, there may be evidence to suggest that nationalism – particularly majority state nationalism – has been strengthened by the pandemic. Bouckaert et al. (2020) note that not only was the initial collective European response quite weak, but there appeared to be an initial nationalistic response which they refer to as 'coronationalism'.

This had led to a particular set of dynamics within multinational states. For instance, while a key element of nationalism is the idea of unity of the national community, Rydzewska

(2021) found that in Spain, while there did appear to be an initial 'rally round the flag' effect, it was short-lived. In the earliest days of the virus, the Spanish government had opted to leave the response to the Autonomous Community governments. A response Sanjaume-Calvet and Grau Creus note was short-lived as the relationship between the central state government and the regions directly shaped the response to the crisis. Similar 'rally round the flag' effects were observed elsewhere, and they were largely just as short-lived (Bouckaert 2020).

Being itself a multinational state, Canada is largely held up as having weathered the pandemic (to date) largely as a federation should – trying to balance both tailoring to local needs with broader coordination, falling short on both counts but finding a sufficient compromise. Note that while calls for fiscal reform, particularly with respect to health care transfers, were present prior to the pandemic, the response to the virus has only reinforced the perceived justification for such reform in the eyes of provincial and territorial (P/T) leaders (Béland et al. 2020). Indeed, at a Premiers summit in July 2022 the P/T leaders were vocal in the demand for reform – calling for the federal share of health care cost in Canada to be raised from 22 to 35 per cent (Zimonjic, 2022). This following what the Premiers referred to as a successful coordination and cooperation throughout the pandemic where the 2022 Chair of the Council of the Federation, British Colombia Premier Jim Horgan held "there was unprecedented collaboration and the federal government was right there and we applauded that engagement" (Zimonjic, 2022).

Throughout, the Prime Minister's office was very cognizant of not reaching too far into P/T jurisdictions, for example being keenly aware of the political risks of implementing the Emergency Powers Act, with the P/T leaders having made very clear they did not see the act as necessary and would view it as an infringement on their competencies (Lecours et al. 2020). The federal government, however, did end up activating the Emergency Powers Act in February in response to a large-scale demonstration of anti-pandemic restrictions and anti-government protests that took over much of the capital from late January to late February in 2022 (Quenneville 2022).

In all, the Canadian case seems likely to result in business as usual, with continued discussion for both fiscal reform and the development of capacity for response among relevant health institutions: discussions that were present and active prior to the pandemic, both within the sub-state nationalist movements such as that of Quebec, as well as more broadly across the federation. In this sense, federalism in Canada can be argued to have functioned largely as it might have been expected – allowing for localized responses, but making coordination more difficult. While there was, what the author refer to as "unity and diversity quality" to the Canadian response to the pandemic, there nonetheless remained classic examples of "blame avoidance or buck-passing dynamics" long common to Canadian intergovernmental relations (Lecours et al. 2022, p.71). This is the textbook trade off of federalism. While there may be repercussions in terms of institutional trust, or political polarization, as a result of the pandemic, the particular functioning of the federation has not been meaningfully put into question either by the state or the minority nationalisms. As Lecours et al. (2022) note "overall, the management of both public health and economic dimensions occurred in respect to the constitutional divisions of power" (p. 69) both with respect to multinationalism as a political institution and as a political culture. The cases presented in this volume demonstrate a considerably different set of dynamics.

While a number of multinational states, including Canada and the United Kingdom, have access to emergency legislation that could have potentially served to facilitate centralized coordination, neither sought to implement it. At the state level, Belgium too was very cognizant of potentially overstepping its authority. While the Canadian government largely operated in a "supporting" role and the British government took a far more laissez faire approach, the Belgian government, as Sinardet and Pieters (this volume) point out, responded to public pressure for a national coordinated response and focused on a cooperative approach that had a de facto centralizing impact. These approaches contrast sharply with the drastic recentralization in the early days of the pandemic by the Spanish government (Sanjaume and Grau Creus this volume), and the overall neglect of Puerto Rico by the Trump administration (Lluch this volume).

The responses of nationalist movements were also impacted by the rhetoric of the central state. In looking at the discourse of state party leaders, Montiel et al. (2021) found that while state leaders in both Spain and Belgium tended to focus their speeches on enforcing systemic interventions, those in the UK relied more heavily on state nationalist rhetoric while the Trump administration, in keeping with Lluch (this volume), stoked nationalist fervour moving closer to populism. Nor are nationalist parties themselves the only ones who may come to see the divides between nationalist communities as more salient during the crisis. Wondreys and Mudde (2022) note that while many parties of the far right in Europe began with an alarmist stance, before walking it back, they soon thereafter started to tie the pandemic to their own pet projects, such as immigration and nationalism. Vox in Spain, for instance, argued that "separatist privilege" was undermining the Spanish response to the pandemic (Wondreys and Mudde 2022).

State	Respect for Multinationalism as Institution	Respect for Multinationalism as Political Culture
Canada	Yes	Yes
Belgium	Yes	Yes
United Kingdom	Yes	Partial
Spain	Partial	Partial
United States	No	No

While the Belgian response to the pandemic appears to have respected multinationalism both as an institution and political culture, it did so in a way that was qualitatively different from that of the Canadian federal government. Whereas the Canadian federal government largely adopted the supportive and coordinating role that would likely be expected in a federal state, the Belgian federal government, at least early on, took a role that was far more involved in the development of consensus between levels of government and in this way took an approach that saw the response to the pandemic as a "national project" rather than as supporting the responses of various regions.

In Belgium, as Sinardet and Pieters (this volume) note, though both policymakers and the broader public are accustomed to a degree of political and institutional complexity, there was a broad consensus that the seriousness of the crisis required a coordinated national response.

The coordinated response that functioned largely on the basis of consensus, put nationalist parties in the difficult position of being less free to criticize federal policy, as it necessarily involved input from members of their own and affiliated nationalist parties at the federal level. Institutionally, Belgium does not possess a clear hierarchical framework between federal and regional governments in health policy, making coordination in this shared competency potentially extremely complicated (Bouckaert et al. 2020). Yet, the very recognition of the highly fragmented nature of health and related competencies in Belgium led to a very clear understanding for the need for a national coordinated response, less a patchwork approach undermine the response to a challenge that cared little for the territorial limits of the competencies of the respective governments (Sinardet and Pieters this volume).

Yet, while the Flemish nationalist movement in Belgium may have found itself constrained by public support for a coordinated response, and so had relatively little opportunity to demonstrate the case for greater autonomy, it is not without means of moving forward as a result of the pandemic. As Sinardet and Pieters (this volume) note, the Flemish nationalist movement was quick to express its discontent at what it perceived as efforts by the federal government to instrumentalize the pandemic through the "team of 11 million" campaign aimed at promoting a coordinated national response. Though by and large, while N-VA tried to argue that the pandemic was proof of a need for a greater devolution of competencies in health matters, the movement remains largely restricted to the political right (Parker 2022), making it difficult to make significant gains.

More broadly, the nature of federalism in Belgium continued to be in question during the pandemic. A key characteristic of Belgian federalism is its fluid and dynamic nature. Even prior to the pandemic, there was groundwork laid in the 6th reform for a broader debate on the federal structure of the country, and in particular, the place of Brussels within that structure. Sinardet and Pieters (this volume) note that the ways in which Brussels' regional government arguably acted beyond its determined competencies may in fact be foreshadowing a new model.

Thus, a notable variation in response is present in what Sinardet and Pieters (this volume) suggest was a surprisingly unified response from the Belgium government. Indeed, while the Belgian response was top down coordinated, it nonetheless involved a significant assumption of major functions by the regional governments, resulting in a response that was more negotiated, delegative and coordinated (Bouckaert et al. 2020). Though perhaps notorious for their difficulties in forming governments in a complex federal system, the political culture and practice of multinationalism arguably facilitated a more negotiated response to the crisis than the drastic recentralization seen in Spain, the laissez-faire attitude of the British state government, or the disregard of the Trump administration for the response to the crisis in Puerto Rico.

In the United Kingdom, a generalized respect for the devolved institutions can be observed, though the degree to which it reflects a recognition of the multinational character of the state as an element of political culture is less clear. The state government largely allowed the devolved governments to operate in accordance with their devolved competencies, with the state government making little effort to centralize control (Parker 2022); a move that, as Basta and Henderson (this volume) note, allowed the Scottish government to demonstrate competence, particularly in comparison to the perceived blasé attitude of Johnson's government. However, while the UK largely showed a clear division of competencies and respect for the various devolved governments, what Basta and Henderson identify as thin political understanding of multinationalism demonstrated by the central state leaves the "spirit" of devolution in a precarious position (Anderson 2022). Indeed, according to Parker (2022) the nationalist movement in Scotland (along with Puerto Rico) is one of few that may have seen some growth in support for the movement as a result of their handling of the pandemic.

Interestingly, while the Catalan JxCat made specific efforts in their discourse to tie their nationalist project to the state response to the pandemic, the Scottish National Party's (SNP's) Nicola Sturgeon largely kept the two issues separate; a strategy that Parker (2022) suggests helped boost support for the SNP. However, while the UK and Scottish responses may not have varied significantly from one another, the perception that they did allowed Sturgeon to demonstrate a competence in governance (Basta and Henderson, this volume) in a way that the high degree of centralization did not allow the governing parties in the Catalan region to do. In a sense, Sturgeon was able to "show not tell", while Catalan nationalist were given little opportunity to "show, and so told" (Parker 2022). In Scotland, the perception of the divergent responses of the SNP and the British state helped garner support for the SNP, with Parker (2022) arguing that such divergence may contribute to increased support for independence. In a widely publicized poll published in July 2022, it was found that 48% of respondents would vote in favor of independence, ahead, but only slightly of the 47% who said no, with 5% were uncertain. While not an overwhelming plurality, many such as Sturgeon herself, publicly celebrated the result given that the inclusion of the "don't know" vote potentially placed the independence side in the winning position in a future second referendum.

Thus, the Scottish nationalist movement was arguably able to instrumentalize its response to the crisis in favor of the broader movement in a way that those movements in states who took a more centralizing approach were not. While it might be expected that the intense centralization of the Spanish state would itself instrumentalize that centralized response to the pandemic for their own nationalist project, the case of Catalunya illustrates that this may not always be as easily done. Although there were efforts by some Catalan nationalist parties to tie state responses to their nationalist demands, as Sanjaume and Grau Creus (this volume) explain, Catalan nationalist were not in a position to take as clear charge of the Catalan response to the pandemic and tie that response to their nationalist aspirations. Further, where as the SNP can largely act as a singular representative for Scottish nationalism, the early days of the pandemic not only saw a hardening of state nationalism in Spain, but a greater degree of polarization within the self-determination movement itself, making a coordinated response by the nationalist movement more difficult. However, this is not to suggest that the Catalan nationalist movement has not sought to instrumentalize the response to the pandemic. While the initial high degree of centralization might not have allowed Catalan nationalist to shine in the same way as the SNP, it contributed to a grievance discourse which allowed the nationalist parties to contrast their stances and policies with those of the central state and make the argument that an independent government could have responded better. In this way, both the Spanish and British state governments provided fodder for the nationalist discourse for the need for greater autonomy.

Moving to a minority nation that received little respect for multinationalism in any form, Lluch (this volume) clearly outlines the disregard for the political, social, and economic well-being of Puerto Rico shown by the US government both before and during the pandemic. Lluch ties this inadequate response and discriminatory response to the needs of the American citizens of Puerto Rican to the broader surge of majority nationalism in the United States that helped drive Trump to the White House: a nationalism of an ethnic bent that imagines the American citizen as a white Anglo-Christian and is hostile to the ideal of multinationalism both as an institutional framework as well as a political culture.

Moreover this response to the pandemic is seen as the latest in a string of federal failures which are viewed as demonstrating a willful neglect of Puerto Rico. In turn, this has contributed to a transformation of nationalism in Puerto Rico as a renewed debate on the political status of the island has occurred (Lluch this volume). This series of failures to respond to Puerto Rico's plight by the US government has culminated in the emergence of new nationalist political parties, a surge in the electoral support for the previously largely marginal Partido Independentista Puertorriqueño (PIP), the election of pro-statehood candidates in the 2020 election, and historic plebiscite where in response to a "statehood, Yes or No" question, the statehood option received a plurality of support for the very first time (52.3 per cent) (Lluch this volume). This is all the more notable given that a pro-independence orientation in Puerto Rico has been always quite marginal and that statehood historically trailed the existing autonomy status as a constitutional option (Lluch, this volume).

Questions over how to balance national coordination and localized responses in a federal state is always a source of potential contention. When the gravity of the pandemic became increasingly glaring and the Spanish state moved toward greater centralization, Navarro and Velasco (2022) note that there was initially little resistance, with the nationalist parties in Catalonia opting to abstain in the passing of the first state of alarm. Yet, Navarro and Velasco (2022) note that following the easing of the initial recentralization of health competencies in Spain, it was not a return to the pre-pandemic arrangements but instead a system which had a greater degree of institutionalized centralization in the realm of health care. The ease with which the state was able to restructure and centralize in the face of the pandemic while it arguably facilitated a coordinated response to the crisis, also meant that the state demonstrated it was both willing and able to run roughshod over established regional competencies (Navarro and Velasco 2022). This tension was only exacerbated by the Constitutional Court's cancelling of autonomous community input into states of alarm. Hence, while it could be argued that the federal systems in German or Canada had withstood pandemic coordination, the "quasi-federal" nature of the Spanish system left regional competencies vulnerable in times of crisis (Navarro and Velasco 2022). Debates about pandemic responses became wound up with debates about sub-state nationalism with some nationalist parties such as JxCat taking a more combative stance, and other such as the Basque Nationalist Party or *Esquerra Republicana de Caluny* (ERC) offering a more cooperative approach (Parker 2022).

The significant structural centralization in the early period in the Spanish response stands as an outlier. In the case of Spain, the lack of an existing framework for vertical coordination in health care between local, regional and the central governments led to an initial reaction of excessive centralization in health care (Navarro and Velasco 2022), which would then have a fallout in the relationship between regional nationalists and the central state. The lack of existing framework in this instance created a situation of significant malleability that allowed the central state to radically centralize in response to the moment of crisis. While centralization was later largely walked back, it demonstrated to sub-state nationalists the fragile protections of their devolved competencies – this not long after a similar demonstration of the clawing back of fiscal competencies through constitutional reform in the aftermath of the financial crisis (Muro 2015).

For Catalan nationalists, as Sanjaume and Grau Creus (this volume) note, there was little opportunity to demonstrate their effectiveness in government in response to the pandemic given, the centralizing approach of the central government.

The parliamentary system in Spain is also one characterized more by an adversarial structure as opposed to, for example, the more consensus focused parliamentary style in Germany (Parker 2022). The minority government of the *Partido socialista obrero español* (PSOE) was reliant on the support, or at least the abstention, of regional nationalist parties in order to pass each state of alarm (Navarro and Velasco 2022). This provided an opportunity for Catalan nationalist parties (along with other opposition and regional nationalist parties) to focus on criticizing the government. JxCat for instance took the opportunity to argue that the lockdown needed to be stricter (a closing of the regional borders) and that an independent Catalonia would have been better positioned to respond.

There was, of course, variation among nationalist parties, with the ERC taking a more conciliatory approach and offering a greater deal of support. Nationalist parties in other regions also sought to take advantage of the PSOE's minority position, with the long controversial party of the Basque nationalist left, Euskal Herria Bildu, arranging an agreement about the repeal of 2012 era labour reforms in exchange for their support (Rydzewska 2021).

This variation in responses of Catalan parties has left the nationalist movement in a difficult position. The pandemic arguably amplified the left-right division in the JxCat coalition, eventually leading to its breakup and the formation of Junts. And while across Spain, nationalist movements have made some electoral gains not only in Catalonia, but in the Basque Country and Galicia, whether that translates into support for independence, Parker (2022) cautions, may not be so straightforward. It may be that parties are being rewarded or castigated for their responses to the pandemic. In the case of Catalonia, while nationalists have, at time of writing, a majority in parliament, there has been no great surge in support for independence (Parker 2022).

The complexities of coordinating a cohesive nationalist response have only been exacerbated by increased polarization in Spanish politics. As Lluch (this volume) points out, majority nationalism has continued to play a role in patterning responses, but it has itself also found opportunities in the pandemic for responding to self-determination claims. While Spain had one of the most stringent lockdowns (Wheeler 2022), parties like Vox on the far-right used the Covid response to highlight their own ideological agenda, such as arguing that the central government was too permissive of Catalan demands (Wheeler 2022).

At the same time, the increased polarization in the Spanish political system was also experienced among Spanish nationalist parties and saw a hardening of positions in the Catalan territorial conflict across the political right of the spectrum. Thus, while the structural changes to the Spanish division of powers may not be significant, the political repercussions will likely be felt for some time. The pandemic highlighted and arguably deepened the deficits of the Spanish territorial system, and simultaneously undermined possible resolutions to the Catalan territorial conflict by altering political priorities, and reinforcing political polarization, making successful negotiations far more difficult (Sanjaume and Grau Creus, this volume).

These varied reactions on the part of the central government raise the specter of a number of potential repercussions. While Canada is unlikely to see any major renovations in the federal structure, nor does it appear to have had any outstanding impact on its nationalist movements as a direct result of the pandemic, the same cannot necessarily be said for the cases explored in this volume.

The pandemic may have given some indication of the direction of the next round of reforms of Belgium's dynamic federalism. In contrast, while little was done in the way of structural changes in either the United States or United Kingdom, the perceived lack of respect for the multinational character of the United States, and the shallow understanding of devolution demonstrated by Westminster may provide fodder for sub-state nationalist movements, either as political parties or as broader movements. Whereas in Spain, the resolution of the Catalan territorial conflict is arguably further away than it was prior to the pandemic.

References

Aguirresarobe, A.H. (2022).. Is National Identity in Crisis? An Assessment of National Imaginations in the Early 2020s. *Studies in Ethnicity and Nationalism*, 22(1): 14–27.

Anderson, P. (2021). The Covid-19 Pandemic in the United Kingdom: A Tale of Convergence and Divergence. In Steytler, N. ed *Comparative Federalism and Covid-19: Combatting the Pandemic*. Routledge, New York, pp. 142–159.

Béland, D., Lecours, A., Paquet, M., & Tombe, T. (2020). A Critical Juncture in Fiscal Federalism? Canada's Response to COVID-19. *Canadian Journal Political Science*, 53(2): 239–243.

Boucher, A., Hooijer, G., King, D., Napier, I., & Stears, M. (2021). COVID-19: A Crisis of Borders. *PS Political Science and Politics*, 54(4): 617–622.

Bouckaert, G., Galli, D., Kuhlmann, S., Reiter, R., & Van Hecke, S. (2020). European Coronationalism? A Hot Spot Governing a Pandemic Crisis. *Public Administration Review*, 80(5): 765–773.

Lecours, A., Béland, D, Brassard-Dion, N., Tombe, T., & Wallner, J. (2020). The Covid-19 Crisis and Canadian Federalism. Ottawa: Forum of Federations and Center on Governance of the University of Ottawa, Occasional Paper 48.

Lecours, A., Béland, D., & Wallner, J. (2022). Reduced Acrimony, Quiet Management. In Chattopadhyay, R., Knüpling, F., Chebenova, D., Whittington, L., & Gonzalez, P. eds. *Federalism and the Response to Covid-19: A Comparative Analysis*. Routledge, New York, pp. 66–75.

Montiel, C.J., Uyheng, J., & Dela Paz, E. (2021). The Language of Pandemic Leaderships: Mapping Political Rhetoric During the COVID-19 Outbreak. *Political Psychology*, 42(5): 747–766.

Muro, D. (2015). When Do Countries Recentralize? Ideology and Party Politics in the Age of Austerity. *Nationalism and Ethnic Politics*, 21(1): 24–43.

Navarro, C., & Velasco, F., (2022). From Centralisation to New Ways of Multi-Level Coordination: Spain's Intergovernmental Response to the COVID-19 Pandemic. *Local Government Studies*, 48(2): 191–210.

Parker, J. (2022). Europe's Secessionist Movements and Covid-19. *Nationalities Papers*, 50(1): 118–129.

Quenneville, G. (2022). Cabinet Told of Possible 'Breakthrough' With Protesters Night Before Emergencies Act Invoked. *CBC NEWS* August 11, 2022. www.cbc.ca/news/politics/canada-cabinet-justin-trudeau-freedom-convoy-emergencies-act-court-documents-1.6548739

Rydzewska, A. (2021). Impact of the COVID-19 Pandemic on the Relations Between Government and Parliamentary Opposition in Spain. *Polish Political Science Yearbook*, 50(3): 41–52.

Wheeler, D. (2020). Vox in the Age of Covid-19: The Populist Protest Turn in Spanish Politics. *Journal of International Affairs*, 73(2): 173–184.

Woods, E.T., Schertzer, R., Greenfeld, L., Hughes, C., & Miller-Idriss, C. (2020). COVID-19, Nationalism, and the Politics of Crisis: A Scholarly Exchange. *Nations and Nationalism*, 26(4): 807–825.

Wondreys, J., & Mudde, C. (2022). Victims of the Pandemic? European Far-Right Parties and COVID-19. *Nationalities Papers*, 50(1): 86–103.

Zimonjic, P. (2022). Premiers Close 2-Day Summit, Call on Feds to Stop Negotiating Health Funding Through the Media. *CBC News* July 12, 2022. www.cbc.ca/news/politics/premiers-secnd-day-victoria-health-funding-1.6518043

Index

Note: Figures are indicated by *italics*. Tables are indicated by **bold**. Endnotes are indicated by the page number followed by 'n' and the endnote number e.g., 20n1 refers to endnote 1 on page 20.

Affordable Care Act (ACA) 84
Alexander, Jeffrey 10
Alexandria Ocasio Cortez 78
American Creed 79
Americanism 76, 80, 89
Anglo-British elites 38, 49
Anglo-Protestant culture 79, 81
ascriptive forms of Americanism 76, 80–1
Australia 22
autonomism 75, 87
autonomous communities 5, 8, 22, 28, 31

Basque Nationalist Party 99
Basta, Karlo 7, 11
Belfast Agreement 37
Belgium 2, 3, 10, 12, 22, 78, 97; centralization and cooperation 58; federal decision-making bodies 58–60; Flemish nationalism 66–8; Flemish-nationalist party 56; fragmented competencies 68–71; multi-national and federal states 55–6; national communication 62–3; national uniformity 63–6; political crisis 56–8; uniform policies 60–2
Biden, Joe 85
Bieber, Florian 3
Bouckaert, G. 94
British Conservative Party 81
British unionism 37, 40
Brussels Common Community Commission 61
Buthe, Tim 19

Canada 22, 40, 42, 78, 96
Carter, David P. 19
Catalan secessionism: pro-independence political chessboard 30–1; repertory of collective action and strategic field 25–6; self-determination movement 23–5; window of opportunity 26–30
Catalonia 1–2, 7–11, 13; and Spain relationship 78; territorial preferences and level of government *29*
cavalry imaginary 18, 31
Centers for Disease Control and Prevention (CDC) 85

centralized Canadian federalism 1
chaotical management crisis 23
Ciudadanos 28, 30, 32
Common Community Commission 69
Concertation Committee (CC) 59
conditional legitimacy 38–9
Congreso de los Diputados 31
conservative dilemma 81
constitutional amendments 4
coronavirus 23, 47–50, 55, 84, 85
COVAX program 94
COVID-19 crisis: governments, parties/individual politicians 8–9; nationalist movement and multinational state 9–11; re-centralization 6–7
COVID-19 measurement: UK, Scottish and Welsh governments **43**
Creus, Mireia Grau 4, 5, 7, 10, 11, 95, 96, 98, 100
crisis management 17, 31, 59

Dalmau, Juan 88
decentralization 20–2, 31
De Croo government 58, 62, 63, 65, 66, 70
deglobalization process 19
deindustrialization 84
depoliticization 60
devo-anxiety 41
De Wever, Antwerp Bart 66
double parity 59
Drakeford, Mark 43

Emergency Powers Act 95
England 8, 37, 40
Eriksen, Thomas Hylland 10
Esquerra Republicana de Catalunya (ERC) 9, 24–5, 27–8, 31, 32, 99
Estado de alarma 33n2
Estado de las Autonomías 20
Estado Libre Asociado (ELA) 77, 89
ethnonationalism 4, 76
European Union 11, 55
Euskadi 77
exclusionary politics 19

INDEX

familles spirituelles 87
far-right ultranationalist party 32
fatality rates 2
federal competence 69
federalism 18, 19, 21, 23, 75
federalization 56
federal system 18, 19, 58, 59, 68–9, 72, 75, 87, 97, 99
FEMA Mismanaged the Commodity Distribution Process in Response to Hurricanes Irma and María 86–7
Fidesz 81
Flanders 2, 8–11, 13
Flemish Community Commission 69
Flemish nationalist party 1, 5, 12, 13, 56, 57, 59, 60, 63, 68, 70, 71, 97
francophone 5, 56–8, 62–5, 70
free associated state 77
French-speaking Community Commission 69

Gao, Rui 10
general elections, Catalan and Spanish Governments *29*
Germany 22, 55, 58
governmental salience 30
Government of Wales Act in 2006 44
Grau Creus, Mireia 4, 5, 7, 10, 11
great union 59
grievance 4, 11, 26–8, 30–2, 98

Hancock, Matt 46, 47
Henderson, Ailsa 7, 11
Horgan, Jim 95
Hroch, Miroslav 87
Hungary 81
Huntington 80
Huntington, Samuel 79–80
Hurricane Katrina 18
Hurricanes María and Irma 76, 83–7, 89

imagined community 62
India 78
Insular Cases 77
intergovernmental relations (IGR) system 17, 18, 20, 22, 31, 95
Interministerial Committee (ICM) 69

Jambon, Jan 66–8
Jenrick, Robert 47
Johnson, Boris 9, 43, 47
Jones Act 85
Junts per Catalunya (JxCat) 9, 24–5, 27–8, 32

Knack 65
Krastev, Ivan 6, 8

Lecours, A. 95
Lee, C. C. 10
Leonard, Mark 6, 8

Le Vif/L'Express 65
liberal integrationism 79
Linz, Juan 78
Lluch, Jaime 4, 6, 7, 12, 96, 98–100
local government 47
lockdown 7, 10, 17, 25–8, 30, **43**, 47, 100

Maestas, C. D. 18
May, Peter J. 19
Merkel, Angela 11, 62
Michel, Charles 57, 59
ministerial decisions 66
Ministry of Defence (MoD) 48
minority electorate 41
minority nations 2–6, 8–9; politicians of 9; and the state 7–8
mission civilisatrice 80
Montiel, C. J. 96
Movimiento Victoria Ciudadana (MVC) 88
Mudde, C. 96
multi-national context 3, 8, 11, 38, 66
multinational democracies 1, 2, 4, 10, 11, 13, 75–80

National Assembly of Catalonia (ANC) 26
national communities 2, 5, 7–8, 10, 11, 19, 41, 81, 94–5
national duality 76
national identities 4–6, 10, 16, 38, 40, 76, 78–82, 89
nationalism exacerbation 32
nationalist discourse 7, 10, 98
nationalist movements 1–11, 13, 95–8, 100–1
National Security Council (NSC) 59–62
natural disasters 3, 76, 77, 80, 81, 84–6, 89, 90
Navarro, C. 99
New York Times 85
Nieuw-Vlaamse Alliantie (N-VA) 5, 11–13, 57–9, 66–8, 70–1
non-centralization 40
Northern Ireland 8, 37, 41, 44–6

pandemic law 66
paradiplomacy 6
Parker, J. 98, 100
Partido Independentista Puertorriqueño (PIP) 88, 99
Partido Nacionalista Vasco 87
Partido Nuevo Progresista (PNP) 87
Partido Popular Democrático (PPD) 87
Partido socialista obrero español (PSOE) 24, 100
peripheral multinationalism 77–8
Pieters, Jade 10, 12
Plaid Cymru 44
pneumonia 2
political polarization 19, 95, 100
Protestantism 40
Proyecto Dignidad (PD) 88
PSOE-Podemos coalition government 26–8
Puerto Ricans 12

Puerto Rico 2, 6–13; distinctiveness of 76–7; national movement 87–9; peripheral multinationalism 77–8; Trumpism 76 (*see also* Trumpism); U.S. national identity, multinationalism and national divides 78–80; U.S.-Spanish-Cuban War of 1898 75

Québec 1–2, 77, 78
Qvortrup, Matt 23

Rachman, Gideon 10
Rajoy, Mariano 24
recentralization 6–7, 22
refederalisation 70, 72
regionalism 23
Representative Nydia Velázquez (D-NY) 87
Risk Assessment Group (RAG) 65
Risk Management Group (RMG) 65, 70
Roularta Media Group 70
Rozell, Mark J. 22
Rydzewska, A. 94–5

Sanders, Bernie 78
Sanjaume-Calvet, Marc 4, 5, 7, 10, 11, 95
Schertzer, Robert 13
Scotland 1–2, 8–11, 13, 37, 38, 41, 44–6, 77
Scotland Acts 2012 and 2016 41–2, 44
Scottish National Party (SNP) 42–3, 87, 98
Scottishness 40
secessionism 10, 19, 25–31
separatist privilege 96
shared-rule 20, 21, 42
Sharma, Alok 47
Sinardet, Dave 10, 12
social distancing 26, 49, 85
Socialist Party of Catalonia (PSC) 9
social media 7, 10, 63
Spain 2, 7, 8, 42, 58, 78, 101; autonomous-community authorities 32; Catalan secessionism (*see* Catalan secessionism); cavalry imaginary 31; COVID-19 crisis 18; Ghebreyesus, Tedros Adhanom 17; literature and theory 18–20; multinationalism and COVID-19 20–3; national diversity 31–2; nationalism exacerbation 32; pandemic management 17; Vox's style of nationalism 32
Spanish Socialist Workers' Party (PSOE) 9
Staatsvolk 78
State of Alarm COVID-19 crisis in Spanish Congress 27, **28**
status quo 9–11, 23, 25, 28–30, 77, 89–90

Sturgeon, Nicola 9, 11
Sudtiroler Volkspartei 87
Switzerland 42, 55, 78

territorial decentralization 40
territorial pluralism 79
territorial preferences in Catalonia *24, 29*
The Times 85
Torra, Joaquim 23, 31
total lockdown 27
Trumpism: COVID-19 pandemic 83–5; ethnonationalism, Puerto Rico 80–2; federal response to crises, Puerto Rico 82–3; Hurricane María disaster 85–7
Turkey 81

unexpected crisis 32
unexpected uniformity 61
Unilateral Declaration of Independence (UDI) 26
uni-nationalism 21
unincorporated territory 12, 75, 77, 80
United Kingdom 2, 9, 11, 55, 58, 77, 96, 97, 101; Anglo-British elites 38; conditional legitimacy 38–9; institutional settlement 41–4; minority/claimant communities 39; minority nations 38–40; multinational predicament 39; multinational settlement 38; multinational state 40–1; pandemic 44–9; political elites 37; territorial autonomy 40
United States 2–4, 6, 7, 9, 11, 12, 18, 55, 58, 101
U.S.-Spanish-Cuban War of 1898 75

Vandenbroucke, Frank 62–3, 67
Vázquez, Wanda 89
Velasco, F. 99
Vergés, Alba 24
Vlaams Belang 11, 68

Wales 8, 37, 38, 41, 44–6
Wallace, Ben 48
Welshness 40
White Man's Burden 80
Wilcox, Clyde 22
Wilmes, Sophie 57
window of opportunity 11–12, 18, 19, 26–30, 32
Wondreys, J. 96
Woods, Eric Taylor 13
World Health Organization 2
World War II 57, 75
Wuhan 2